Build Your Village

How to Build Your Sovereign Village Coop

Build Your Village

How to Build Your

Sovereign Village Coop

Itančan Wašaka

Build Your Village By Itančan Wašaka

Published by:
Pueblo Press
677 Cash Street,
Croydon, NH 03773

Interior Design by Pueblo Press

Cover Design by Pueblo Press

ISBN:

Contents

Be the change you wish to see in
the world.

– Gandhi

Author's Preface

I am passionate that we thrive when we live with others who support us. I meet many many people who want a different kind of social structure – a new society. But no one seems to be

> ***This book shows the best practices in building your village, balancing cost and function.***

able to figure out all the pieces to do it. Having spent years with numerous communities with varying amounts of success, I have extracted what seems to work. These are the best practices of the successful. I will keep updating this book and the best practices as we all learn more about what works well in various circumstances. You can also see details at the Forums (Knowledge Base) at RBEV.org,

Furthermore, my interest is in fully collaborative communities that build their community together with the principles of Resource Based Economics. This is in sharp contrast to many so called "Intentional Communities" most of which are designed principally for cheaper housing to varying degrees. They may be Home Owners Associations, Condo Associations, or Co-housing Groups. To my mind, they are elaborate neighborhoods. This to be sure is a community. It is **not** a RBE Village. It is not a Coop village.

An RBE Village is a shared community that is self governing and manages its resources collectively. They are best structured as a cooperative non-profit village. It can, with work, rise to the level of a wealthy micro-nation, an independant enclave.

A heart based unifying tradition seems critical. It binds people together. This is commonly a religion, a political belief system (as in militia groups) but it can also be spiritual practices and values. Personal responsibility is key here. It is also business based.

A separate village can easily turn into a cult over time where the members are subject to tremendous peer pressure to go along with everyone else. It becomes quite difficult for someone to leave. Guard against this. Let everyone be their own sovereign. The only rights anyone gives up are those they consciously agree with. No one is forced or pressured to do anything. No implied consent.

When I started this book it was called ***Village Economics*** because the finance and economic operation of the village was of crucial importance.

Having participated in numerous intentional communities, I saw that many failed. Some may argue that they still continue, so let me say they did not meet the goals of their founders. They muddled through barely making ends meet, and making very few happy.

So I started researching the success of intentional communities. There are numerous scholarly works that seriously dug into this. In short, they concluded that it was easy to understand the incredible failure rate that nears 100%, although some notable exceptions did succeed, usually because they were very well capitalized ionitially, but I again argue that is not a good success criteria for evaluation.

There are numerous challenges to creating a village.

The top challenges are:

1) Creating a vibrant culture based on trust and love.
2) Creating a fun enjoyable environment.
3) Working together collaboratively.
4) Making enough money to more than merely survive.
5) Handling the social issues in moving to a new paradigm without money where much is shared.

All are significant challenges. Keep them in mind as you read this book.

#1, creating a **vibrant culture** based on trust and love is the most significant, so I will cover it at the end of this section. Trust is a challenge in our western cultures.

#2, a **fun enjoyable environment** is the result of meeting all the other challenges when you maintain this as an ultimate goal. You can meet the other four challenges without creating a great environment. It must be deliberate. This takes planing and attention.

#3, **working together collaboratively** is paid lip service by many people. In reality, few are equipped to really do this, and do it well. The current western culture support individualism and consumerism. When you move away from that, it feels at first uncomfortable. It shows up as fear in most people. They are not comfortable relying on others for backup or help, as a necessity. They view that as optional. It is easiest to think of collaboration as like what occurs in a close knit family. It doesn't occur often, but when it does, it works. We can all understand that. Family members can count on each other to be there when needed. Family members do not need to actually like each other to do this. They just have to be willing to stand up for each other.

This is similar to many military squads. Each member would die for the others. They don't always like everyone though. You must start with this idea to achieve high collaboration. Everyone must buy into "We have each others backs." You do not have to like each other, but you do need to commit to be there for each other through thick and thin. It's easy to say, harder to do.

#4, **making enough money to survive** is elemental. Most businesses fail which is routinely estimated by the SBA that 90% of startups don't last ten years. A village is not just a business, but much more. No wonder so many fail.

Even more so, many intentional communities start on a very egalitarian concept with the idea that the money will take care of itself. Most of the people involved have weak, at best, concepts of how business works. In my years with the Small Business Administration (SBA), I saw many many entrepreneurs who started with a minimal understanding of making money. They had no idea of how to evaluate a business. They just looked at popularity or customer count. True those are important, but most of this style do not make good money. Plus they tend to be labor intensive (its a lot of work for many people).

Take restaurants. There is a reason banks rarely lend to startup restaurants. They are a huge challenge to make good money. It is possible. It is never easy. It

It is easiest to think of collaboration as like what occurs in a close knit team.

takes a lot of capital for both the equipment, furniture and fixtures, site buildout, and inventory if you just rent your space. That is just to start. Then you need a huge staff so you struggle to pay adequate wages usually with no benefits, and struggle to retain them, while getting rid of the serious losers.

Managing costs is also difficult because margins are razor thin. A chef I know once told an apprentice "There are over 100 ways to cook onions. The way I told you is most efficient. I don't care if you can cook them 50 other ways. After 20 years of trying all the ways, I know this specific way is fastest, cheapest and creates a great result. Do it my way." Managing cooks is challenging. Egos get in the way.

Just like producing a great book is more than selecting high quality paper, a good restaurant is much more than cooking high quality foods. That is basic. Chefs who focus on the food usually have terrible restaurants because they do not give adequate attention to all the rest.

Yet, the average person seems to think restaurants are a good business. It is most often a high passion.

It rarely is a good business. Even when it is, it is challenging to make good money.

Many business work like this. They may be fun for the owner, but they do not produce good money, particularly when given a high capital investment.

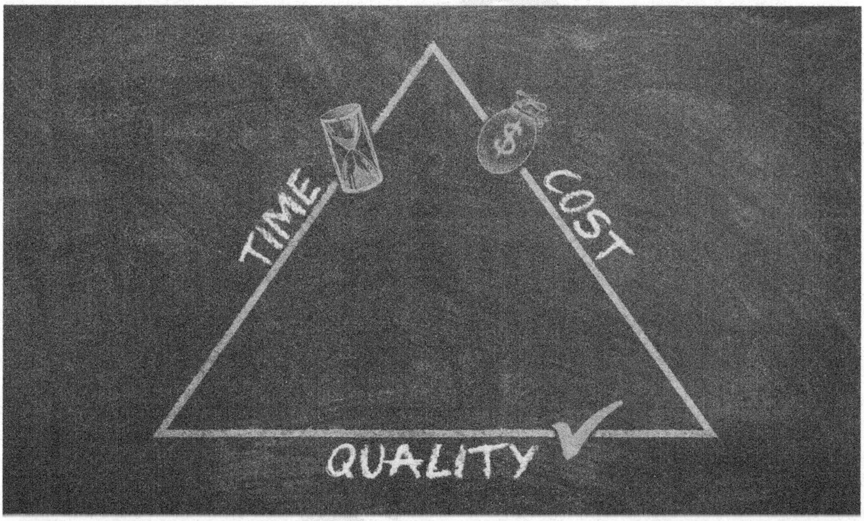

So, when starting a village, select its core business with great care. Have someone lead the effort that understands business in depth. If you do not have anyone, do not start until you do. It is not someone who understands accounting or bookkeeping. Most are too caught up in the details of record keeping to be good at analysis, except that with lots of public experience, they see what works and what fails. They do see the returns. They will not be of much help though in a really new, different, or disruptive business.

Good business people understand business dynamics. They also understand accounting and finance. Good accountants do not necessarily understand business. They understand financial record keeping.

In fact, within the accounting profession, they distinguish between Custodial Accounting and Managerial Accounting. Custodial Accounting focuses on what happened and proper record keeping and reporting to the various statutory authorities. Providing accurate records with three years of history by month is what they do. With a nonprofit coop village, we seek to minimize the record keeping requirements.

Select your early businesses carefully to be sure they can return enough surplus to run your village.

Managerial Accounting instead focuses on running the business. While history is helpful, you do not lead by looking in the rear view mirror. The province of Managerial Accounting is projections and forecasts. Are your projections and forecasts based on data and information, using good math. While there is some art to this, there is also much math, financial math. The more you can know what will happen, the more exactly and effectively you can plan the use of your capital.

A village needs Managerial Accounting far more than it needs Custodial Accounting. The later can readily be hired out, usually for small money, if no one in the village wants to do it. Surprisingly (to me), some people love this work of entering data and keeping records. Most people are surprised that although I love financial strategy and planning, I hate accounting and bookkeeping. It's just not fun.

So you need a business that inherently can make good money. You also want a business that is needed. You also need to be able to compete. To do so, be clear on why you will win. This is called differentiation. The stronger it is, the better you will do. Without a significant advantage, you will just battle it out with your competitors and struggle to make money. Since they are better known, all else being equal, they will win far more often. Spend a lot of time on this selection in the beginning.

#5, social issues and Members social skills also play a critical role. You do not want to be constantly in conflict banging heads. People who cannot handle their own fears easily, will create problems for the group, especially when they are in leadership roles.

Use financials to help you run your village rather than simply keeping good records.

It is common when seriously changing your operating paradigm, for irrational fears to come up in the most rational people. Expect it to happen. Again, expect this to happen to you too. Plan for it. Know what you will do. Support each other when this happens.

The unfamiliar carries with it big fears. Things just don't feel "right." Be patient with people. Openly talk about it. Share fears and share how you handled your fears. Make it good to discuss fears with others. Recognize that often objections to decisions are based on these fears. Risks get exaggerated. When people cannot speak calmly about a decision, recognize fear is likely at work.

Supporting each other in managing your fears in a new environment is critical.

Lastly, culture is the set of values and ritual practices the village holds important. Key values should be written down. I found a good practice is to turn the core values into a pledge that is recited ritually at the beginning of each meeting. Clearly it should be relatively short and highlight the key values of the village. The ritual recitation keeps it fresh in peoples minds, and anchors it with new members. This helps make your values and principles real, not just another plaque on the wall. Supporting each other in managing your fears **in** a new environment is critical. Don't let this catch you unawares. Be prepared.

Starting your own village has significant challenges. Naturally, a lot of good sound communications is required. The outcome however is an amazing place to live, that feeds your soul and raises your spirit.

Itančan Wašaka

Summary Points

- **The top challenges creating a village are:**

  1) Creating a vibrant culture based on trust and love.

  2) Creating a fun enjoyable environment.

  3) Working together collaboratively.

  4) Making enough money to more than merely survive.

  5) Handling the social issues in moving to a new paradigm without money where much is shared.

- To collaborate with your village you need to develop trust.

- Plan your businesses to earn a surplus to run your village and gain wealth over time.

- Use financials more to manage your businesses and village than to keep a financial history.

- Managing fears is an important aspect in changing your paradigms in a major way.

Live simply that others might

simply live.

- Elizabeth Ann Seton

Introduction

This book is directed to those who want to move outside conventional society **now** into the new world enabled by democratic high tech capabilities. You first moved outside conventional finance, fiat currency, by embracing Blockchain crypto. Now AI has cme along and offers greatly reduced effort to the most tedious and mundane tasks. Open Source is creating applications and designs that are shareable.

Similarly, you can move your legal affairs outside local jurisdictions with a complex sovereign trusts that work under common law, at the same level as the constitution, above statutory jurisdictions. This is the realm of nations, which includes micro-nations.

Take a minute and let that set in.

It is at the common law level that you create the legal structure for your own village, a self-governing

> You are moving outside traditional money and outside traditional structures to self-governance.

cooperative, starting with a few friends and family members. You start the village with 6-10 homes at the most on beautiful rural land. That is enough. These households are your founding members. You can start with some investing members who move there later. This gets a greater number of homes on the property early on. These Founders determine the character of the village culture.

Cultures and organizations can be of several types. For example …

- Set up legally as a corporation, LLC, or irrevocable trust. A formal cooperative is best for community governance which can usually be done under any of these legal structures. This varies by jurisdiction. In a coop, all Members are equal owners.

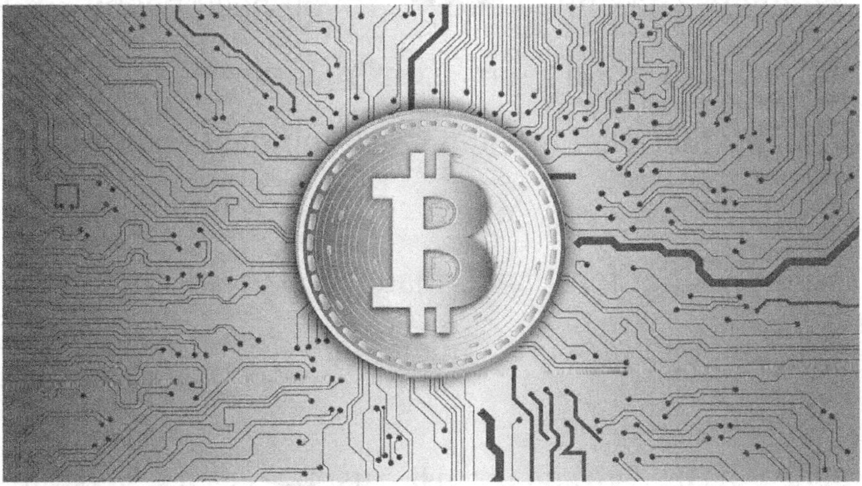

- Governance can be autocratic like a corporation, or a democratic collaborative. I recommend democratic where everyone gets heard. That is most satisfying to all concerned.

- Simple or complex in its workings.

Many are prepared to help you all along the way through a nonprofit, the RBE Village trust. It does not charge for planning, organizing, governance, strategy, setup, construction scheduling and financial strategy. The only charge is if you need people to go on site to train your construction team. That is usually included in the predevelopment costs of your project anyway, much like Architectural and Engineering fees, and made a part of the overall housing and property financing.

The RBE village trust itself is a Separatist Organization that exists outside conventional statutory jurisdictions. It is self-governing and is setup as a Resource Based Economy (www.resourcebasedeconomy.org) utilizing Regenerative Economics or Donut Economics (doughnuteconomics.org). It is for people who want to live with others they are close to, in harmony, close to nature and outside the consumer culture. The village exists beyond the "Consumer Economy" and internally does its own banking and operates without money day to day. A treasurer manages and operates externally with other jurisdictions and nations on behalf of the entire village. All is done openly within the village.

> By using a cooperative structure you **facilitate** member ownership and democratic governance.

A Village Coop starts out as an investment where the adult Founding Members put in capital and share operating expenses. Realize you are investing in the development of a new community village. You are building your own town and eventually a micro-nation. This investment is shockingly small though.

As an example, ten two bedroom cottages plus a large community center can be constructed for about $350,000. Land can be bought and prepared for another $150,000 to $250,000. A mortgage on this would cost about $3,500 to $4,200 per month for the village or $350 to $420 per household. You build them yourselves, but it is surprisingly easy. Three average people new at it can put up (frame) one cottage in three days. More details to follow in this book.

Monthly expenses for the village vary but are not all that high. These costs are divided over the adult members rather than each household. The village can decide how to apportion the total costs so it is fair to everyone. Typical costs run $300-600 per month. Food is the biggest part of the overall budget, but it also includes utilities (electricity, propane, water), Internet access, cell phones, computing costs (tablet or laptops), cost of village vehicles with insurance and fuel, etc.

A village is an investment by the members, particularly the Founding Members.

If the village goes into farming and/or animal raising, the food cost can be reduced. But, be forewarned, it is less than you think. While the results are “free,” you need substantial money for seed, fertilizer, farming equipment, barns, animal feed, and animal processing fees. The net gain, if any, is pretty small. But you know what you are eating, and it will be much fresher, taste way better, and be more healthy than anything you can buy.

Find a nearby farm that can supply you with what you cannot do yourself in either meats or produce.

So, this means if no one puts up any capital, a household would pay the $500-600 capital plus $300-600 per household adult member for the first few years. While hardly free, it is very low cost. Moreover, over time the cost quickly goes to zero! The village is an investment that soon pays off.

The financials are highly specific to the village details. The first thing to do is create a plan. I have seen villages cost even less that I am qupting here.

Within a few years, if desired, the village income can rise to the level of self sustaining where members no longer need to cover expenses. Within five years, if a goal, the village can develop its core business to raise it to financial independence and make a profit for its members. This is where there is more than enough surplus money to cover the village cash needs to deal with the world outside the village.

Five years is pretty fast to create your own village from scratch! And when you get there, it pays you as you live there. Within the village no money is needed. Most purchases are made by the village rather than the individual.

Summary Points

- The village is self governing and runs without money within the village. The village pays for all.
- A village treasurer handles external affairs (outside the village) on behalf of all members.
- A cooperative structure enables democratic governance where each member is an owner.
- One way to start is to invest $600,00 capital, or a $300/month mortgage per home, and $300-400 per month living costs each per adult member.
- You start a village with investment and grow to self sustaining over five years or so.

I. Pre-Development

Being organized isn't about getting rid of everything you own or trying to become a different person; it's about living the way you want to live, but better.

- Andrew Mellon

Village Building Process:

How to create your own village.

The overall process of building a village is broken into numerous steps as follows.

Preplanning: 6-9 months

1 Create your village concept.

2 Find the core Founding Members.

3 Decide if any virtual village members.

4 Agree on village concept.

5 Create capital plan for village & business.

6 Assess each member's capital input.

7 Develop funding strategy.

8 Create initial operating plan for village.

9 Determine roles: Village Chair, GM, Treasurer.

10 Do initial work plan from each Member.

11 Develop implementation time line.

Acquire Property: 3 months

12 Find suitable property.

13 Determine infrastructure needs.

14 Update capital plan.

15 Purchase property.

16 Schedule building materials deliveries.

17 Setup temporary living on property (in RV campers).

18 Move onto property in RVs (Core Team).

19 Start weekly Village Council meetings.

Build Village: 4-6 months

20 Develop property roads and utilities.

21 Build in utility lines to each home location.

22 Begin initial cottage construction – two teams.

23 Team one frames houses including utilities.

24 Team two follows completing the interiors.

25 Team one constructs Community Center.

26 Team two completes interior of Center.

27 Use Community Center for meetings, offices.

28 Both teams build remaining cottages.

29 Move into cottages as soon as ready.

30 Continue use of RVs for guests and visitors.

Begin Village Operations: 3-4 months

31 Update work plan and budget.

32 Get village vehicles, equipment, electronics.

33 Develop plan for village businesses.

34 Appoint Business Leader.

35 Create team to build business facilities.

36 Create team for fardening/farming. Set schedule.

37 Build business facilities (rentals, office).

Full Village Operations: 18 months later

38 Start village rentals with a few buildings.

39 Expand rental cottages as you grow.

40 Start marketing for business customers.

41 When ready, start business operations.

42 Update work plan for steady state operations.

43 Revise long term capital and ops plans.

The length of each of these groups of steps is, of course, dependent on what you are exactly doing. The time estimates are just to give you an idea. It is critical to plan for the business, as well as plan the village. This business is the economic engine that will drive financial independence. The longer you wait to start it, the longer it will take to get independence.

Notice that during the first year on-site, the routine will keep changing. You first have to arrange temporary living on site, usually with campers and recreational vehicles. Everyone need not come onto the site immediately, just the construction teams.

Realize each Member's daily routine will change frequently, monthly, in the beginning.

Construction will occupy the weekly activities for some time as you start with infrastructure, and move to building construction: the first cottage or two to learn what to do. Then shift to the Community Center so it can be used. Finally complete the cottages so everyone can move into the village.

Once the housing is done, it is time to start the farming, if you cannot do it sooner, and build the rental housing or business facilities depending on what business is decided. If the business is online, it may start in a Community Center office and expand out later.

With all the advances in AI apps, many services can be offered remotely, from the village. These can be Virtual Assistants, Financial Consultants, Bookkeepers, Creative Services, Social Marketing, Campaign Marketing and Management, Creative Writing, Book Editing ,,, the list is endless. Use the whole team in the village. Some do the actual customer engagement, others do the connection with prospects and interested parties, others do promotion, and others do customer satisfaction validation and testimonial gathering.

The weekly Village Council meeting is critical to stay on track and make sure everyone is involved. Much fine tuning will be done during this setup period. Keep the meetings short and on agenda. Provide advance materials for any topics requiring understanding.

This is an "operational" meeting. It's purpose is to make critical decisions and review progress on goals. Discourage "chatting" or the meetings will go on for hours and you will lose members. Keep it to the business meeting agenda.

You can socialize before and after. Dinner after is a common approach since everyone is there. Do socializing during that time.

If everyone works to keep the meeting on topic, it can be very short and engage everyone.

Summary Points

- Members daily routine will change each month during the building phase of the village.
- Use your village council to stay together and on track. Keep the meetings short and succinct.
- Socialize after the meeting to discuss issues that arise.

The way to get started is to quit talking and begin doing.

- Walt Disney

The Village Coop

Why set up the village as a cooperative

A Village Coop may start and stay small, or rise to a maximum of 50-60 residence homes (200-250 people) whereupon is is time to start another village. Many communities limit the size to 50-60 adults so everyone is very close. Below 250 total people, everyone knows each other personally and politics is minimal. Sociology shows us that over that size, people break into clusters where the people no longer know each other well. This results in the expansion of distrust and politics in daily life and operations. Politics expands exponentially with population size. Maintaining the culture becomes very challenging. It is easier to just start another village.

It is far more effective for the village to support the creation of an affiliated village not too far away and support its development. The established village can provide some or all of the financing for the new village, ideally at zero interest. It can go further, based on the desires of the existing village members, to ensure the rapid rise to the financial independence of the new village.

When starting a new village, go through the full startup process. Don't shortcut things. Whoever will be the Founding Members must be carefully selected. They need to do a full work plan. They can call on the experience of the existing village, and thereby save some time. However, it is a new village and as such needs its own plan and strategy. Existing village elders should take the role of advisors only, letting the new Founding Members make their own decisions. It must be their plan.

Keep the village small 50-60 people, with a max of 250, to keep it fun and non-political.

Keep the village small 50-60 people, with a max of 250, to keep it fun and non-political. The new Founding Members may be either new Members, who want to join this new village, or existing members who are up for starting the new village.

When starting a new village, the current village would then have the vacated homes of those leaving for the new village to "sell" to interested members wanting to join the current village. This would take the form of a Membership Fee, to join the existing Cooperative. There is no profit. It is merely what the selling Member originally put into creating the village, if any capital was put up initially. This should be spelled out in the rules of the cooperative.

To be clear with an example, say a village has reached a peak of 30 homes. The Village Council decides that is at the maximum population the village wishes to support. Members from four households are interested in moving to a new startup village. Their home would be then vacant in the current village and available for others to move into with their investment. That investment rather than being returned to the departing Members, instead goes to the new village to pay for their share for the new housing needed in that village, which is a new legal entity. They lose their equity in the old village but it is replaced by theat of the new village. As there is no capital appreciation in a coop, and all members have one share only, there is no financial difference.

Start the village with 5-10 households and anchor the village culture strongly.

In a cooperative, the surplus is allocated at the decisions of the Members in their annual planning. Since it is a nonprofit, distributions may go to members after all Village needs are considered. These may be increasing expenses for various items, or purchasing additional assets like vehicles and equipment, or investing in another business, or finally creating or expanding a cpiital fund.

Since all housing and land is owned by the Village Coop, individual houses are not "owned" and thus cannot be sold directly. It all goes through the Village Council.

Why Create a Coop Village?

The overall objectives behind a village coop is to support:

1. Living in a beautiful natural setting, while doing activity that is fun for each person, with lots of free time;
2. Living in a supportive community where resources are shared so everyone benefits and creates wealth together;
3. Living outside the stressful consumer economy, in a community where money plays a minimal role, getting even less over time.

People, creativity, expertise and resources are valued, not money, per se. Plans strive to keep all in balance. This is what a Resource Based Economy is all about. One approach to do this is called a "Donut

Economy." Amsterdam is an example of a large city that has adopted this approach. It seeks to balance resources with needs. Think of your coop village as a small micro-nation. Outside your village is another country. You need money for foreign exchange and trading. Within the village you do not. The Treasury Staff manage the foreign trade and money. No one else need be concerned.

Be sure to look where your community and your environment is going over the coming decades to avoid catastrophic disruptions.

The annual planning is what helps keep everything in balance. The purpose is to be clear where the Members need to put their attention in the year ahead to meet their needs. The Members decide as a group. Hard trade offs need to be made between resources available and income generated by the village. As you can see, good planners, financial strategists, and business people are critical to success. While straight forward, success is not an accident. With financial growth, it gets easier.

Because the village is self contained, once self-sufficient it can deal with change more readily than conventional society. But it is not immune. Look at all the disruptive impacts on society already. Part of planning is to look ahead and anticipate what is coming. Plan on how the village will address the change.

Is there some new technology the village will forego? Despite the post pandemic massive movement out of the cities, it is not as radical as first thought. Most are merely moving into a greater ring around existing cities. Suburbs are transitioning to "exburbs". Expect an increasing difference between city living and rural living. These village coops work best in a rural beautiful natural setting.

In a village coop, people are free to pursue their interests while work is minimal. The work is what one chooses because it is rewarding and fun. Tasks are not assigned but requested. If no one requests to do certain tasks, people to do them must be hired from outside. With community maturity, undesirable work gets smaller and smaller, and may be readily hired out.

The way a Village Coop evolves is based on the strategy for the village in conjunction with the skills and desires of the Founding Members. The Founding Members set the values and culture of the village. Once set, a group's culture is difficult to change. Be as deliberate as you can.

Summary Points

- Start the village with 5-10 households and anchor your culture.
- Limit village size to 50-60 people optimally, and never over 250 to minimize politics in a fun environment.
- Plan far down the road so you can deal with major changes you see coming in time to minimize disruption in your village. Plan to adapt.
- Make sure you plan the village activities so everyone is having fun doing work they love.

Don't waste your life

– sign on Zen monasteries

Cooperative Living

Why live cooperatively rather than individually?

The overall objective is to live simply, close with nature. The emphasis is on acquiring long lasting quality goods that are needed, and sharing items not constantly needed. Equipment that a typical homeowner owns may be owned by the village instead, eliminating the need for everyone to own it.

For example, this is a good way to treat personal vehicles. It saves Members money each month while avoiding a parking lot full of seldom used vehicles. Insurance is cheaper on a fleet policy also. You use Village Gas Cards for fuel. Maintenance is either done locally or in the village if one of the members is so skilled. You just run it like zip cars - sign up and go.

It is preferable to start with raw land that has no structures on it. This will be the cheapest. You get the most for your money this way. The tradeoff is the village can be operating faster with existing structures. In all cases, additional homes will be needed. Simple homes are recommended with a basic half bath (toilet) and a kitchenette, since major facilities will be in the adjacent community building. A shower in each cottage, particularly for outside workers (construction and farming), can easily be added if needed at low cost. Water availability is usually more the issue. This will maximize the space within each home. Combined with high ceilings of 8’ in the back (bedrooms) rising to 12’ at the entrance, the space seems surprisingly large.

The home design supported is of variable size, but typically with average 10’ ceilings. The higher ceilings add very little to the overall cost. This makes any space seem much larger and more livable. Home designs are, of course, up to the Founding Members and later the Village Council.

Homes can be simple 36 x 24’ two bedroom cottages, 10’ high, that feel quite large.

Cabins, the size of an RV, can also be done at, of course, much lower cost (half), with 8’ ceilings and a flat roof. This flat roof can be decked, which is ideal for scenic locations such as in the mountains.

A common cottage economic size is 36’ x 24’ which allows a great room with a kitchenette on one side plus dining and lounging area, plus a half bath, and two or three bedrooms. Although a shed roof can have a loft at the 12' end, it is more cost effective to just make the building larger to accommodate additional space needs.

Home construction uses a proprietary Post and Beam insulated panel approach available through the RBEV.org at cost. These panels are used for floors, roofs, exterior walls and interior walls. Exterior walls are 8" thick, while roofs are 10-12" thick. The panels are up to R7.5 per inch of thickness or R60 for walls and R90 for roofs.

The panels have a quite minimal off-gassing, and none when sealed, which is a requirement. You do not want the panels exposed to sunlight directly. It deterioriates them.

Panels are custom manufactured in 8, 16, and 24' lengths each 4' wide. The panels are high tensile strength highway foam normally used under major roads particularly before bridges. This is not insulating foam, which has no structural strength.

These panels are very strong and can handle loads much greater than concrete. They are also a reusable resource. Because a wall is just 2 or 3 panels high, by laying them sideways, three trained people can completely construct the house shell easily in three days. With experience this can be reduced to two people over two days in the later stages of village construction. RBEV.org can train you as part of the project. Learning is very fast, as you can imagine.

Panels with a concrete stucco finish were extensively tested to building standards specs. See CTI Specification at RBEV.org forums for test results.

Once framed, you cut in conventional doors and windows. Electrical and water lines are run through the walls. Then the interior can be completed including interior panels for room partitions. These need not be more than 3-4” thick, yet will provide high sound absorption between rooms giving much privacy within the cottage. Interior and exterior walls can be finished off any conventional way.

Panels have minimal off-gassing, and once sealed none at all. The panels are forever. If the house is no longer needed, the panels can be readily reused in another house or the current house moved to another location where needed. If you do not need the panels, some other village will want them.

An air based geo-exchange can maintain a 70F temperature year round with no electricity, just using vent windows.

All homes and cabins have solar panels, controllers, and batteries, usually 200-300 watts. This is enough for 12v lighting, a 12v apartment refrigerator, and charging electronics for computers and cell phones. These homes are completely off grid, except for backup when batteries are not enough, as in northern winters. You can also supplement off grid with propane on-site electrical generation if needed.

HVAC is relatively easy. The cabins have R60 walls and floor with a higher R90 roof. They maintain internal temperature easily with minimal additional heating or cooling. EarthShips has over a decade of testing fresh air pipes in the ground that comfortably maintain a year round temperature of 70F without even fans, using passive solar heating and venting it. Two 10” HDPE culverts 30’ long under the 1465 ssqft house bring up ground temp air (55-65F) which can easily be heat pumped or augmented to comfort. This also allows good air exchange in the home as well. Fresh air flow is important for a comfortable living environment.

Home designs also include both a small wood stove for ambiance and backup heat, or use a propane RV heater as a safety backup for extreme weather. It’s not needed except to deal with people’s fears. It’s the space heater solution. Once you know your winters, you can stop buying them and even sell off your excess.

A simple sewage approach is to use a holding tank with a pump out capability. Only put toilet outflow into it. All else is gray water.

Sewage is done by first separating gray water (sinks and showers) and black water (toilet). Usually, gray water is merged with black water and then sending all output into sewage. Gray water is 80% of conventional output. So a more effective and environmentally sound approach is to have gray water piped into outside gardens. This is good for plants. The remaining 20% black water is handled various ways. This is much more efficient.

Rural jurisdictions will commonly allow just the holding cistern without a leech field if the tank is large enough. This is commonly done to save cost. It is also better for the environment without the large leech fields. A conventional holding tank will not need a pump out for 5-10 years, and then probably nothing will be left but dust – so no pump out will actually be needed. This is a holding tank just like campgrounds use for campers and RVs.

If you host RVs on your site, you can also provide a pump out station for their sewage. Just make sure that holding tank tank can accommodate the RV pump outs.

Cabins can have a high end composting toilet which needs no plumbing. A Home Depot model only needs emptying every 3-6 months with a family of four. Then it is just fly ash which makes a great compost in the non-food gardens. This then avoids the septic tank entirely. This will be an argument, however, with most jurisdictions, even though it makes sense. They are afraid of composting toilets. Rural jurisdictions tend to be more lenient and understanding than municipalities.

Alternatively, toilets can be sent into a sewage storage tank and pumped out as needed. A large cistern tank may only need to be pumped out every ten years if that. That saves leech field installation.

Community Center toilets can be done the same way. Either they are composting toilets or they sent into a sewage storage tank and pumped out as needed.

Alternatively, EarthShips has a design for an underground waste water treatment tank 20 x 40' that is self contained and needs no maintenance. Plants grow on top. It is serious construction though. You may want to add it later as the village grows. It's a lot to take on in the beginning.

Water is done in a variety of ways. A well is ideal, especially for potable water. In arid locations, where water is scarce, it can be hauled to the site and dispensed for potable water. While commonly cheaper than municipal water charges, it is another task the village needs to deal with. Rain capture is also a good option if you design with sloping metal shed roofs and send it into a common cistern that feeds everyone. Use a simple solar pump, or a water tower so it is gravity fed like many towns do.

As you look at your possible property consider what you will have to do for all infrastructure: electricity, HVAC, water, and sewage. These services need to be brought to each building. If you have grid electricity, municipal water or sewer, or gas, they all need to be brought onto the property and then run to each building. Plan carefully as these runs can be very expensive.

For off-grid, propane generation is a cost effective option for backup electricity as well as cooking and heating backup.

Cooking is most easily handled with a large propane tank initially, and used only for cooking and HVAC backup (minimal in sunny areas). A large tank is filled once or twice a year. This is a good solution for the first decade. In the longer run, extreme low cost solar can provide induction and convection cooking energy.

Biofuels is a short term alternative, but sources can be difficult to find. Biogas from digesters is another approach. Although it was very exciting a few decades ago, the results have been questioned. They take up a lot of space and are unsightly. Biogas is basically captured animal farts. Is that what you want to cook with? It's not my choice.

The Community Centers serve as the social hubs of the village. Have at least dinner there daily, to bring everyone together. Its a simple opportunity to connect and maintain community cohesiveness. Breakfast and lunch are more often informal. A simple oatmeal or pre-made breakfast can be done early each day and Members can just east when they want. Lunch can commonly be leftovers from the previous days, reheated as needed, also.

Each Community Center decides what works best for itself. Shopping, food preparation, cooking, cleanup, and dishes are all tasks that need to be shared in the village work plan. When done well, everyone doesn't have to be involved with everything. With income growth, people can be hired if desired to do some of this work also.

The key to making everything work is the semiannual work plan. Each member commits to what they will do for the community, which is accepted by the community, and then whatever is undone is hired out. The first plan is most difficult because everyone is starting from scratch and people's desires are unknown in the beginning. The plan differs significantly with each season, and with construction projects in parallel. In addition, the business may be seasonal as well. So the plan must be seriously updated at least every six months. Each Member's commitment to their proposal is the key to making this work.

Summary Points

- Villagers share resources to reduce overall costs. This is a good way to handle vehicles.
- It is most cost effective to buy raw land and build.
- Small 2 bedroom cottages are an inexpensive good looking homes, villagers can quickly build.
- 200-300 watts, through batteries, is sufficient solar for a small cottage fridge, electronics, and lighting.
- If water iw a challenge, consider rain water capture with an elevated cistern. Also look at hauled water for the cistern if needed.

- Separate water into gray water and black water. Only black water goes into the septic system.
- For septic, rather than leach fields use a pump out station and only put toilet output into it. It will go years without needing emptying.
- Gas is the best way for cooking and backup heating. With a propane generator, it can also be inexpensive electricity during low solar activity.
- A Community Center is a great structure to pull the community together for meals and gatherings.
- Make a labor plan by season and update it often during the initial years.

Successful investing is about managing risk, not avoiding it.

- Benjamin Graham

Investing

How much do you need to invest to start a village

It takes investment for several years to build a vibrant strong village coop, along with its core businesses. Figure on five years or so. During this initial period, Members have paid in Capital for housing, and monthly "rent" to cover living expenses and any loans on the real estate. Housing capital and loans are apportioned over the ten houses and monthly expenses are apportioned over each adult Member (i.e. over 14 years old). This can be shortened if you can raise enough initial capital to build housing faster. I have seen typically at 30 cottages, where 50% are rentals, you can earn enough to reach break even. This can be done in three years.

Clearly founding Members will need some outside income or savings. It does not take much, but something is needed. The more capital members are able to put in initially, the lower the monthly costs since there will be smaller loans to pay back.

Members are not paid, and there are no jobs. Members share the work of running the village and its core business just like a large family, certainly in the beginning. Each adult Member proposes to the Village Council what they will do as their working contribution, and the Village Council agrees. If no agreement can be reached, that person can not included in the village. They add insufficient value during the startup phase. Every member must pull their agreed weight.

Consideration is given for young children, older less able adults, those disabled, and those with illnesses. You might minimize those who cannot contribute significantly at the very beginning and bring them in later. Just all agree how you will do it. Be thoughtful. Imagine if we discarded Dr. Stephen Hawking because he was a fully paralyzed. He went on to make major contributions as a leading physicist for decades. Everyone has value. Find it.

A household can submit a proposal for the work that all of its adult members will perform, of course. Ultimately, the Village as a whole must agree and accept the offer from each Member as worthwhile. This is the core agreement of each member or household with the Village. If at any time it stops, and no further agreement can be reached, then the household or Member must leave the village. To not enforce this will seriously undermine the village operation. To be able to count on each member is critical to successful operations. Without this, the situation gets increasingly difficult. Needed tasks do not get done. The village is all about collaboration.

Central to reaching financial independence for the village is the development of at least one core business that is strong enough to actually sustain the village. Remember, it is the net profits that the village can use to pay its outside bills, not the business' income.

While some businesses are important, they are not strong enough to also pay the bills. A good example is farming. There is very little profit in farming – ask any farmer.

> **Each village member proposed to the others what results they will get done for the village.**

However, it gardens and farms can offset food costs while providing much higher quality desirable foods. Raising your own produce, fruits, and animals is about the quality of the food far more than economics. It will also raise the work level substantially, if you are trying to make money doing it. Farming will not be fun for many people. In any case, start small and grow into it. Make sure you have enough people who love farming and raising anumals. It can be labor intensive, and animals are fed by sunrise and at sunset.

The Village core business needs to do some economic activity that produces a cash surplus (net profit) which goes to the Village. This surplus is initially used to make loan payments (mortgages) and pay monthly operating expenses thus decreasing the monthly "rent" requirement on each Adult Member and household.

Eventually, as the village business grows, operations will create a surplus greater than the needed monthly operating expenses and loan payments. Then the Village Council should have a plan on how to handle the additional surplus. This can be additional capital investment and/or Member stipends. Member stipends are cash payments to Members for use outside the Village (vacation travel, medications, clothing, etc.). This can start at a few hundred dollars per month and grow. A common maximum is $2,000 monthly. All adult Members receive an equal amount. For people doing exceptional work, higher amounts amy be given as approved by the Members.

A profitable money making business is the backbone of village economics.

Remember, the philosophy of a Village Coop is to live simply close with nature. Life should be simple and fun. You work at what is fun for you. New members are particularly brought in over time to meet specific skill requirements.

All Adult Members are free to propose purchases to be made by the Village. The Village Members all vote on this bearing in mind if it is in the existing budget or not. This can be anything from recreational equipment (Spa, sauna) to heavy equipment (tractor, truck).

Resources are shared across the members so money is not needed within the village. Included within the Village Coop legal structure is a Financial Trust which can do banking functions for the village. The Treasurer will determine the banking capacity based on the economic activity of the Village.

Resources are shared across the members so money is not needed within the village.

Members may get loans from the Village Council or invest their stipends at the Village Trust until needed. Working with Wise.com, DebitCard accounts can be maintained for each Member for easy access, once they are needed. Wise.com can maintain funds in over 40 currencies with minimal conversion fees.

A village trust can be set up to provide banking type financial services to members.

For the more adventurous, off shore operations, can provide crypto currency accounts totally outside the current financial system. This is best interfaced with Wise. It is not easy and the financial tracking laws are working hard to prevent this. But, it is an eventual option.

Summary Points

- Villagers each propose to the group what results they will deliver as their contribution from the list of work needed. It must be agreed worthwhile by all involved. The work changes seasonally.
- The village needs a core business that generates enough over expenses to sustain the village itself.
- Rental housing is one good way that is not labor intensive and can generate a lot of income.
- While food is essential for well being, it is not a strong money maker. It does offset food cost.
- There is no need for money within the village itself. Banking services can be done for dealing with the outside world.

I have seen that in any great undertaking it is not enough for a man to depend simply upon himself.

- Maȟpíya Lúta (*Red Cloud*) Teton Sioux

Legal Structure

How to legally structure your village for maximum protection

A Village Coop is ideally legally structured into multiple Non-stock Corporations and Common Law Sovereign Trusts.

The Non-stock Corporations are used by each organization requiring a bank account. Most or all are setup as non-profits. Where useful, an IRS registered 501c3, non-profit is created. This means it is able to accept tax deductible donations. This company does not pay taxes. You can make one a 508c1 which is a religion. They are automatically granted with no requirements on any specific beliefs.

Then you do not pay property taxes either, and no one argues. However, it is not as strong as a 501c3.

All other organizations are Irrevocable Trusts. It is generally not required, necessary, or advisable to register the trusts with anyone. This avoids registration, renewal, and annual reporting fees. It also makes the trusts harder to find which gives the village additional legal security. The exception, is you register the trust as the owner when you register real estate.

The US Constitution is at the same legal level as Common Law. As jurisdictional law derives from the Constitution, it sits below them in legal hierarchy. Common US jurisdictions are Federal, State, County, and Municipal. A sovereign irrevocable trust is at the same level as the constitution.

The proper venue for hearing legal issues between US entities and foreign sovereign jurisdictions is the District Court of the United States in Washington DC, the so called "Article III Court." This is where an issue between France, for example, and a US entity would be brought.

It takes specially certified lawyers to appear before this court. They are very expensive. Only nations can appear, so if you have an issue with a state, they need to get the federal government to appear on their behalf. This is enough to get many to drop the issue. Municipalities and states usually first try to bring it to the courts they know. You move to dismiss the case as improper jurisdiction. Jurisdictional issues must be heard first before other motions. The court needs to be sure they are the correct jurisdiction.

In all courts, motions on venue must be heard before all else. If the judge refuses to hear it, or denies it (don't be surprised here), you have clear grounds for appeal. You will win on appeal.

All this is why trusts provide greater legal protection and lower costs for setting up a village. Don't go looking for fights though. They are long and protracted. Just don't give up your rights actively. You are outside the conventional jurisdictional legal system, so you will be pretty much left alone. The key is establish your village as its own sovereign jurisdiction.

The Village Coop itself is setup as a non-stock non-profit corporation in the local jurisdiction. It handles the external bank account for paying monthly bills. It owns nothing except its operating cash. It is the operating organ for the Village Coop. All regular activities are handled through the Coop.

Irrevocable trusts combined with noon-stock corp's form the legal structure of the coop.

Separate independent trusts are then created for each asset class: real estate, vehicles, equipment, securities and investments, and a fiduciary trust. Each trust is relatively non-active with a separate board (may all be the same people though). Each is not legally connected to any other organizations. The trusts limit legal liability and exposure, all trusts being independent. Separate businesses, when large enough, may be set up as separate non-stock nonprofit corporations as well. Surpluses are reinvested for the benefit of the village Members.

For example, if the vehicles are all in a vehicle trust, then any law suit arising from the use of a vehicle can only sue the vehicle trust. The maximum award will be the equity of that trust plus its insurance. If you minimize the trust equity, the maximum loss is just the insurance payout. The same is done for other trusts, like a land trust, an equipment trust, etc. There is one or more trusts for each asset class.For example, a restaurant may have multiple legal entities: an operating non-profit, a real estate trust for the property, and an equipment/fixtures trust for the restaurant.

The Fiduciary Trust then liens out the value of any asset trust tat has equity. That is, they put a loan on the trust that removes all equity formally on the books. This ensures there is not equity in that trust. If legal action is taken against the trust, there is no net value to gain. This seriously discourages legal action.

This complex legal structure provides much legal protection , better than insurance.

There is no value to get from the owner, the trust. If there is also no insurance, no lawyer will likely take the case because there is no one with any money – not the owner, not insurance. This is particularly useful with real estate holdings.

The Fiduciary Trust also provides Village banking kinds of transactions such as loans, to Members, recommended interest free. It is not a registered bank though, merely a fiduciary trust thus avoiding banking regulations. Initially the banking functions are minimal in the startup phase. As time goes on, especially when Members receive a stipend, the banking functions become more important to facilitate dealing with the outside world (other nations and micro-nations). Within the village (a micro-nation itself) no money is needed.

If not yet obvious, a Village Coop is a move beyond the conventional "consumer economy." Consumer spending is a clear addiction, and can be very difficult to move away from for many people. This is important to take into consideration with the Founding Members. Shopping and fast online shipping is a major source of uplift for many people. So, make sure all new members understand this and are prepared to handle it. If not, major conflicts will erupt after you start.

Another change fear that arises is property ownership. When everything is owned by the village, the individual owns little except what they had before coming to the village. They do have an equity share of the village itself, but it is a

cooperative and shares do not appreciate. The gains go to the village coop itself. The equity share can be set by a Membership Fee in coops. When someone leaves, that Fee is returned. Membership fees need to be carefully thought through. One way to do it is to set the fee at the cost of housing capital per household.

During the startup phase, the members must pay monthly expenses and provide capital or sign for construction loans.

A Member may join and provide some cash and take on the rest as part of the debt. When they leave, they are entitled to the cash they provided plus credit for the principal of their share of the loan payments. Every new member then pays in the same membership fee. The village can discount an existing cottage to make it more attractive to a new member or just let them have another cottage built to their specs.

Summary Points

- Villages are structured as nonprofit corporations and irrevocable common law trusts for maximum legal protection, and minimal insurance costs.
- The legal village structure is complex but only needs to be done one time.
- During the startup phase, members must invest capital to setup the village or sign onto loans or mortgages for that amount.
- During startup, the members must also share the monthly living expenses in addition to paying off loans for the property and construction.

It"s not hard to make decisions when you know what your values are.

– Roy Disney

Work Planning

How to plan the work of the community

Central to the effective operations of a Village Coop is the work plan. This is a series of commitments by each Member to the Coop, to what they will do each week, that is accepted by the Coop. This is critical for the Members to know what they can count on from each other to get done.

In each community there are several kinds of work to plan. They are: 1) Running the Community itself, 2) Running each village business, 3) Construction Projects, and 4) Special Projects as they arise.

Running the community consists in all the village direct activities such as cooking, getting food, cleaning up and dishes, cleaning the group buildings and community center, landscaping, firewood, snow removal, and raising food and animals.

Additionally, staff may be needed for each business the village operates. If for example, you rent out housing you need people to clean the buildings after use, check people in and out, register people staying, routine maintenance and repairs, etc. For people on long term stays (months), this may not take many people very much time.

When you start, there will be much construction to do building the homes and community center. After that, you may want to build extra buildings for rental income or a village business. This takes labor and needs to be included in the mix of work.

Lastly, you may have special projects requiring many to pitch in working like planting a fruit grove, or installing a new sewage pump out station. Don't forget these either. Plan four seasons in advance.

There are four kinds of work in the village: 1) routine operations 2) the village businesses 3) land development and construction 4) special projects to develop the village.

Initially, list all work activities that need to be done by the village and the approximate amount of work involved. All adult Members then propose what they will do for their share of the Village Coop tasks both each week, and seasonally. If their proposal is accepted, it represents a strong agreement with the Village, and may only be changed by subsequent Village Council agreement. This is a crucial step. Each member needs to know what they can count on others to complete. When someone does not do their share, it ruins everyone else's morale and attitude.

Each villager proposed to the others what they will do during each season. It is accepted by the members at large.

Any Member who repeatedly does not keep their agreement is subject to removal from the Village. It is important that such violations be quickly and decisively dealt with. Not keeping agreements quickly undermines cooperation within the coop.

As an exception, if someone breaks an arm, they may not be able to keep their dish washing commitment. They need to propose something else to the Village Council for the interim period. It just has to seem reasonable to the other villagers. Keeping agreements is central to collaborative village life. So is understanding each member as an individual. It is all centered around clear agreements.

In another vein, seriously disruptive people also need to be quickly dealt with. This is not a disagreement between Members, but rather

consistent bad behavior that disturbs most other Members. This is a frequent occurrence in communities and must be addressed quickly. A socially disruptive Member must be removed. The Village acts together, but if the process is dragged out with multiple warnings and behavior doesn't significantly change, village morale and cohesion will significantly suffer until others leave because they cannot stand it. See it coming. Act quickly.

Once you decide to act, it may still take 30-60 days to remove someone from the village. One single negative person can destroy the fun and joy of living in a village.

Summary Points

- There are four kinds of work in the village: 1) routine operations 2) the village businesses 3) land development and construction 4) special projects to develop the village.
- Pay people to do the work that is not covered by the member agreements.
- Each member proposed to all others what they will do by season. The proposal if accepted is a binding agreement with the Village.
- Expect the work plan to shift by season and by year during the development cycle.
- Because of all the change, long term seasonal planning is critical.

Three frogs are sitting on a lily pad.

Two decide to jump off.

How many frogs remain on the lily pad?

Three, two decided, but didn't act.

- Brian Tracy

Village Council

How to govern and run the community

All adult Village Members (over 14) are initially Members of the Village Council. It is the operating body of the Village Coop. **Its purpose is to review proposals and to make timely decisions, as needed.** It is not for communications. Use other forums for keeping people up to speed and connected.

The purpose of the Village Council is to review proposals and make decisions.

They elect a chair with limited powers, if they feel they need one, to organize the weekly Village

Council Meetings. Commonly, an elder just does it by general agreement. There is no power here other than keeping the meeting timely and on track.

The role is to set the meeting agenda, run the meeting, and keep to the agenda. They also call special or emergency meetings. Since most meetings are weekly and routine, the work is largely to set the agenda for each meeting, and keep everyone on track during the meeting.

The real skill of the Chair is to guide everyone to make a decision where everyone can support the decision, even if they prefer something else. The key question is "Can you live with this decision." More on this approach is contained in the materials on Dynamic Policy Governance. The principle is that unless everyone can go along with a decision, it is not agreed. This approach lets everyone's voice be heard and provides great coherence among Members.

Use task forces to implement proposals. Fully empower each member so no review is needed, just periodic updates.

The purpose of the Village Council is to make all major Village Coop operating decisions, unless delegated to a subset of members in a task force. This is very unusual and will usually be for an issue that concerns only a few members, the rest being indifferent to the outcome.

More commonly, a task force will be impaneled to gather facts to make a better decision and report back to the Village Council. For example, before making a decision on buying a farming tractor, a small group may be sent to find out the various options such as a used tractor for a farmer, or from a dealer, or rentals.

Summary Points

- The purpose of the Village Council is to review proposals and make decisions.
- Keep the meeting short and decision focused. Do a social hour after the meeting to discuss issues.
- Use task forces to implement proposals. Fully empower each member so no reviews are needed, just periodic updates.

Schools teach you how to work for money, but they don't teach how to make money work for you.

- Robert T. Kiyosaki

The Village Business

How to decide on your village business.

Each Village Business is set up in a way similar to the Village Coop itself, as a set of separate legal entities. Each distinct business also needs clear management, elected by the Village Council, that acts as their Management Team. Once their annual plan and budget are approved, they operate independently, except for reporting back weekly or monthly.

A common good starting business for a village can be local worker housing. There is high need in most rural areas. Most rural housing is priced very high, beyond the reach of workers. Where do the workers live? Choices run from poor to non-existant. This commonly limites the economy of nearby communities. Since they have nowhere to house their workers, getting employees is challenging, if not impossible.

Since the Members will become experienced building their own cottages, they may want to build more and rent them out for income. These rental units are usually in a separate area of the property so as to be away from the village itself, with separate road access.

AirBnB is a good way to manage rentals, even monthly rentals, because it avoids all the issues of landlord laws. It operates under hotel accommodations rules, so putting someone out is simple and quick. Dave, in Groton CT operates 50 houses this way with great success.

Over time you can build additional rental units for additional income to the village. The profits can also fund additional village housing as additional members join the village.

Carefully select your initial village business to generate an adequate income to run the village with its initial members.

You rent month to month. Naturally, you can offer some units for shorter stays, but much more work is involved. You have to clean the unit after each stay, and replace the linens. Linens are not provided for monthly rentals unless requested. People bring their own for longer or indefinite stays. Because you are using hotel accomodation laws, you don't worry much about getting paid on time. This saves much hassle and Member time managing the rentals.

In short, you may have many units rented by the month. Others, at a higher daily rate, are for tourists and visitors. Just fit your offering to the demand in your area.

With beautiful rural property, many people will want to do a get-away in your area. Don't forget, the day rentals will need housekeeping in addition.

Most rural areas have a chronic shortage of worker housing. Since you only have materials costs to cover, you can rent at the bottom of the local market to ensure you are fully occupied and still make good money for the village.

Summary Points

- The most common effective income generator is rental housing. Get enough initial capital to build additional housing that you can in turn rent out.
- Most rural areas are very short in worker housing. What is available tends to be very expensive.
- Rental housing has a low labor requirement so it frees members to do the activities they love.
- Select your initial village business carefully. Maze sure it can generate the fund needed to sustain the village early on. Expand it over time.

If you don't go after what you want,
you will never have it.

- Nora Roberts

Startup

What getting started is like, the timeline

It is best to start with **5 households** as a practical minimum. You need a variety of skills, especially for both construction initially, as well as food production. Do not start with over ten — it is too cumbersome to start with more homes. Pick the ten strongest households to start. Every adult over 14 is expected to contribute their time to running the village. This is not likely to be much of a burden if everyone cooperates (less work than your own single household because work is shared). You will need to build one home per household plus a community center (say 30 x 50’). Materials can be purchased through RBEV.org to save money. In addition, RBEV.org will train village members on-site in housing construction. Members may volunteer at other sites to learn the skills in advance and minimize RBEV.org time on-site, if any.

Building construction is easy to learn by any worker with rudimentary skills within a few weeks. While not necessarily involving everyone in the village, it is a major village project and everyone who can gets involved. Typically three people can put up a home in three days. Land prep, and interior finishing are additional time needed. The house designs are usually quite simple to minimize construction time. Once completed, they are beautiful. Most houses are basically a box with six sides. For variety, a bump out can be designed in to provide a bit of extra space at minimal cost or labor.

Start with five to ten households, not more, not less, to effectively anchor the village culture, values, and work program.

Land preparation is dependent on the property acquired. The work falls into these areas:

1 **Electricity**: do you have electricity coming up to the property? If so, what is the cost and work to bring lines into the property and up to your buildings. If the village is far from where the nearest pole is located, there can be considerable cost. You can run lines yourself using a trenching tool to bury the cable and have an electrician

certify where it connects to the pole and at each building. If you do not have electricity nearby you will need an alternative. This can be solar with batteries in most areas. A propane generator backup is recommended for full off-grid locations. Co-generation may be a preferable option using gas, even when the grid is accessible. It can be cheaper, especially in sunny climates where solar is available during most days.

2 **Water**: will you be connecting to a municipal water system nearby? If so, you will need to run lines from it to your buildings. More commonly, you will not have water pipes nearby. So you will need a well. In some areas permits are a big deal so check first. If a well cannot be done for either expense or permit reasons, you can "haul water." Have the potable water you need delivered to storage cisterns. This is usually surprisingly cheap. The rest of your water may be able to be supplied by rain capture.

3 **Heating and A/C (HVAC)**: The RBEV.org (RBE villages Trust, a nonprofit) designs have major insulation which requires very little to maintain ambient temperature inside. With that, a GeoAir approach, pioneered in Earthships can be used. This is a 10" culvert 30-40' long under the

building with an intake outside for fresh aid, and a register at the other end inside the house. Then with vent windows up by the 12' roofline in Taos, Earthships have easily maintained 70F year round with the addition of passive solar windows but no power needed. A simple wood stove or propane camper heater can always be used as backup.

The RBE Villages Trust provides no cost support, coaching, and planning assistance.

4 **Sewage**: This is usually the most challenging issue to deal with due to often stringent local regulations. You can most directly put in a septic system with a leech field. There are simpler approaches though, which separate gray water from black water. Most locations allow a large septic tank with a pump-out but no field. This is much cheaper. You can set it up using black water only so you do not need to pump it out more often that 5-10 years – i.e. never. Earthships have also developed 20' underground waste treatment ponds that have no smell and biodegrade naturally.

5 **Roads**: If not already there and usable, roads will need to be cut onto the property to get to the housing areas. Try to place the village parking outside the main housing areas to minimize roads and village traffic. No parking by the houses themselves. Keeps the air cleaner near the houses also. Think about using the road in all seasons, particularly winter and spring mud seasons. Make sure you can get out if you need to. This can be a considerable expense if you do not select your property and site location carefully. Because roads tend to be long, even a simple dirt path can be expensive. You'll need to hire a catapillar for a few days or more. You may be able to delay road work to the second season or later.

After initial infrastructure and housing construction, additional on-going work will be required for two major areas: additional housing construction, and village business operations.

In a Village Coop, work is divided into task results (outcomes) without assigning hours. Everyone who signs up to do a task, takes on completion of that task as their commitment. For example, one agrees to cleanup all the dishes after a meal on alternate days, not to do dishes for two hours. When estimates are in error or shift, the Member goes back to the Village Council and changes their commitment with the agreement of the Council.

Acquire the land needed, at least ten acres, and plan the infrastructure: roads, water, electricity, sewage, and heating and cooling.

Some Members may do well working outside the Village, in other jurisdictions, earning money there. For those who want that, there should be a clear agreement on what their fair share is to pay-in weekly, in addition to the monthly fees so that someone can be hired to do their share of village tasks they will not be otherwise available to do. They should at least do something on the weekend though (25% work level) to be an active part of the community.

This would be the case, for example, with a medical or dental practitioner wanting to set up an office in a nearby community say three days per week. Their pay would be theirs, not going to the village. Then other Members decide what would be fair for them to contribute. They still have two days available they can work in the village.

When feasible, you could also set up their office within the village in their own building, or part of a community center. Then make the practice a village business. When this is the case, services to villagers can be made free, as would be normal. You may decide to pay the healthcare worker more than an average stipend.

They keep the income they earn unless the Village gets involved in their business by providing space or support. Then it turns into a Village Business.

For example, a dentist may wish to have an office in a nearby town. He may then pay the Village $400/week to cover shared work. He tends to the food gardens on the weekend.

Build a community center and one cottage for each household. You can build these.

Later on, as the village grows, he may want to have his dental office in the village. Then the village will invest in a dental office, the equipment needed, and some of the Members may support the dentist. He may see outside customers in the village. Income then goes to the village. The dentist would then stop paying the extra he had been paying because the dental work is now village work.

The general concept is that people offer to do tasks that are fun for them. When the tasks have no takers, then the Members must decide to either share the drudge tasks among themselves or hire someone to do it.

The Village Coop is a member based cooperative following the international principles of cooperatives. A major element is each member has one share of ownership in the coop village. All members have equal shares. It is not freely sold like stock though, but they may get bought out if they leave. Members also get one vote in all Membership voting. No member may have more than a single share. For more on coops see the ICA website at: www.ica.coop/en/cooperatives/what-is-a-cooperative

The Village Coop operates with the surrounding communities as a separate nation. This is like foreign exchange with another country to meet their needs. Your village deals with the US, for example, just like Canada or Mexico does.

There is no need for currency within the village. Currency is only needed outside the village. The village works over time to maximize its balance of payments in its favor through its business enterprises. The economic transactions are all handled by the Village Treasurer.

Village Development Stages

Villages develop in three stages: 1) Investment inside the village. first two years; 2) Balance and Growth years 3-5; Financial Independence after year 5 or so.

Stage 1 involves Members contributing capital to build the village and its infrastructure, as well as start the village core business, and “rent” to pay monthly bills. Founding Members must have some financial means either capital or passive income during the startup phase uintil the village becomes self sustaining.

Stage 2 occurs when the village business produces enough profit to pay all village expenses. For cottages, the only question is cost. It is very easy to get carried away with interior upgrades. These discussions can be challenging. Just remember that each household should cost about the same to be fair, allowing for family size. The Founding Members set the basic standards and options for interior design levels and quality. Also, the member may later leave the house, and it will later have to be paid for by someone else. Block undesirable or costly designs. Decide as a group what you all agree upon.

Founding Members provide the capital or hold mortgages on their share of the project. The village pays off each mortgage.

At this point it costs Members nothing to live in the village. As profits build, the village enters **Stage 3** where it has more money than needed for operations. The Village Members then prioritize what to use these funds to do between additional business expansion, Member Stipends, or eventually starting another village when Membership gets large enough.

The capital cost to startup a coop village is the funds to purchase and prepare a large tract of land plus construction of the first ten homes and the community center. Then monthly expenses are shared among the adult members. The typical capital investment required is about $600,000 or $60,000 per household. That covers $300,000 to buy the land and install infrastructure, and another $300,000 for construction materials. It can be done for less, but that is a good starting point for planning.

Members are shown how to build the homes themselves as a team so the only cost is materials, and these costs will be one third conventional construction costs through RBEV.org. Designs are simple and high quality. Any design can be built.

So the investment per household is $60,000 in this example. That can be provided as a cash contribution to the Village Coop or that member guarantees a mortgage on that $60,000 investment.

Common needs are $300,000 for the land and infrastructure, and $300,000 for the community center and 10 cottages.

An additional investment initially of $300,000 is recommended to build an additional ten cottages to be used as guest rental housing. This starts the village generating income immediately. Once the villages have built ten houses, ten more is surprisingly quick. The rent pays off their short mortgages.

Monthly expenses typically run $300-400 per adult Member. If the capital investment is all borrowed rather than supplied by the household, the additional loan payment will be about $400 on a current 15 year fixed mortgage for that household.

Capital Investment can be accumulated with a one time membership fee per Member. The fee is decided by the Members but should allow enough capital to begin. The fee is returned if the Member leaves the community.

Members may leave and cash out their membership contribution (be refunded). They may not sell to another existing or new member. That is up to the Village Council to ensure new members fit well within the social structure. All property is owned by the Village Coop. It is the village that pays of the loans over time from its business earnings.

Bear in mind that the structure of the initial capital is a decision made by the Founding Members. The easiest way is to find sponsors for the mortgages and land. This could be Founding Members themselves who hold the mortgage loans. The Village owes the loan, and makes the payments. A separate land trust owns the property itself.

Summary Points

- Start with five to ten households, not more, to effectively anchor the village culture, values, and work program. If less, get to ten quickly to have the skills the village needs.
- Acquire the land needed, at least ten acres, preerably 100, and plan the infrastructure: roads, water, electricity, sewage, and heating and cooling.
- Build a community center and one cottage for each household. Members can build these.
- Founding Members provide the capital or hold mortgages on their share of the project. The village pays off each mortgage.
- Common needs are $300,000 for the land and infrastructure, and $300,000 for the community center and 10 cottages.
- Add $300,000 more for investment rental income generating units.

In order to change an existing paradigm you do not struggle to try and change the problematic model. You create a new model and make the old one obsolete.

- Buckminster R. Fuller

Financial Stability

How to achieve financial stability

At the heart of every successful Village Coop is a reliable business that produces good profits. Starting any business is risky, as the 90% entrepreneurial ten year failure rate would suggest. Select your core business carefully. Understand how your business makes a profit. This is called its business model. Be aware, many active businesses make very little profit.

One reliable business opportunity is rental cabins. After the village has constructed ten homes for themselves, they will be skilled in this construction approach. They can buy materials at cost through the non-profit Croatan IC, and receive technical guidance, planning support, and capital access.

Since they can build these homes for between 15-20% conventional costs, they can undercut the local housing market. In most areas, particularly rural, there is an acute shortage of homes to rent that are affordable for workers. Most people charge high prices.

Since the houses are brand new, they will command top dollar. Price them below market to keep them full. You will have a waiting list for occupants. You can rent daily, weekly, or monthly, and price accordingly. Remember you need to plan for cleaning and housekeeping after each rental period unless the tenant is long term.

Rental cabins are an effective initial business to start that you can grow.

Rent through AirBnB. With the right pricing, they will always be full. However, the regulations governing AirBnB are those of hotels, not landlords. This necessitates month to month rentals. If someone doesn't pay, they can be evicted easily within days, not the elaborate tenant eviction procedures governing landlords. This makes management much easier.

Ideally, rental housing should be developed on the property, but away from the Village itself. It can easily be monitored by dedicated Members. Housing can be augmented with amenities for workers (ride shares), seniors (scheduled trips and rides), Vets (resident social workers), etc. The Member workload is relatively small consisting of admin, routine maintenance (initially minimal), and augmented services.

Particularly poor choices for a village business are food based enterprises. Farms are difficult, challenging, labor intensive, subject to weather, and particularly low profitability. Many many farmers do not break even. A profitable farm must be quite large.

Similarly, restaurants are notoriously low margin, with high staff requirements, and capital intensive for kitchen equipment. These may be fun things the village wants to do, but it is unwise to plan on making a lot of money on them, certainly not enough to run a village. By all means, sell what you don't need or donate it to a food kitchen in the area, or give it to neighbors.

Rent through AirBnB both long term and short term for maximum flexibility.

Growing food is something each village should consider to provide a reliable source of very healthy produce and meats for the village. At this level it is not too difficult, and offsets the monthly food expense. Free range farm animals can also provide needed protein in addition to hunting on your land.

Other businesses are based on the skills of the founding and joining Members. Online businesses are particularly appropriate where a few village members can handle marketing, admin, and fulfillment from online sales.

Health care services can be very effective when combined with Integrative Medicine and Holistic practices. It has the added benefit of being available to the village also.

A health center can combine housing for residential stays with Integrative Medicine, holistic, and natural medicine treatments for chronically ill people to give their bodies a chance to rest and recover for fairly low costs. This looks like a good business opportunity.

Vehicle and equipment rentals is another easy way to make money. To do this, you need a Member or two who are very good at finding things cheap. Instead of renting construction or farm equipment, buy it off season for a good price and rent it out locally when you are not using it. Resell it when you are done with it in-season for a profit. This is a great way to offset costs. It would have to be quite large to support an entire village, though. This is good for leveraging capital.

Automobile rentals can be set up similar to equipment. Buy cars at auction for very low prices. Do whatever cosmetic work is required to be usable (village Member?).

A health healing center is an idea that works for people with integrative medicine skills that is a great social benefit.

Then put the vehicle on the Village Group insurance policy. You can then rent the car to people who need a car for work but cannot afford too buy one. Rent it by the month and include the insurance, and all maintenance. Give your long term renters priority for these vehicles. Require service every 90-120 days. You do the service and include it in the monthly price. This way you can make sure the vehicle is well maintained and that the renter is not abusing the vehicle. As a business, you need a good vehicle mechanic and a garage facility in your village (build one).

In all cases, check out the local market to be sure your business can produce a significant surplus.

Summary Points

- Worker rental cabins are an effective initial business to start that you can grow.
- Rent through AirBnB both long term and short term for maximum flexibility.
- A healing center is an idea that works for people with integrative, holistic, and natural medical skills that is a great social benefit.

II. Build Your Village

Treat the earth well: it was not given to you by your parents, it was loaned to you by your children. We do not inherit the Earth from our Ancestors, we borrow it from our Children.

- American Indian Proverb

Land Acquisition

How to find the right property

In planning your village, the total acreage and terrain of the property will limit your size. A configuration of 20 homes and a community center can comfortably be tightly placed on a flat three acre parcel. They can be in a figure eight configuration with the community center in the middle of the eight – two loops of ten homes.

However, in most rural areas, land is very inexpensive, ccrtainly compared with urban towns and cities. Unincorporated county land is best because oversight is minimal. You will be less subject to zoning regulations.

When looking, we recommend you look at anything over 20 acres, but particularly at least in the 80-100 acres so that you have room for some expansion as well as privacy. When looking, the natural beauty is important. It is wonderful to have great views

everywhere you are on the property. It is also nice to wake up each morning with a gorgeous view outside. In the mountains it can be a great vista, and in the forests it can be a lovely landscape.

Two sites that can help a lot initially are: Zillow.com and Realtor.com

Both allow you to select type of land. An old building may be useful if it doesn't add too much to the cost, but it usually does. It may also take a lot of labor to fit up. That said, it can be used for temporary living space while doing the initial building, then become an outbuilding, community center, or storage barn, later.

> **Rural land is the most cost effective approach with the greatest value.**

Remember, you can get cheap recreational vehicles (RV's) with sliders for very little (we spend $1,500) off season. They make great temp living, being fully equipped, during construction. They are also good construction offices. One with a living room slider makes a great office, conference room. The back bedroom can be converted to another private office.

Land acquired should have as few encumbrances as possible, particularly avoid an HOA (Home Owners Agreement). Ideal land is outside municipal jurisdictions on county only land. Building and land ordinances are usually a minimum. Land will be usually zoned farm or agricultural land.

There is much large acreage available as more and more people move away from farms and ranches unable to run them. These properties are more expensive but will have some or all infrastructure already included needing usually minimal updating. This includes electric power lines into property, water from wells usually, septic systems to accommodate existing building, and, most of the time, existing buildings to get housing started. A farm house can be the good basis for a community center with guest bedrooms and office space.

There is a large supply of ranches and farms owned by seniors whose children do not want them. It is a bit of a problem in rural America. There are good land deals to be had. They usually come with infrastructure all developed.

Rural land is plentiful as most people still want to be near the big cities for jobs.

Undeveloped land means you will need to run electricity as needed (or be totally off grid); drill wells for water, and install septic for sewage (or water treatment facility). While this can be expensive, the land cost will be much much lower. The investment will be likely comparable to a ranch, and often lower in aggregate.

Environmental considerations: Look at the local history of environmental dangers such as forest fires, earthquakes, high wind storms of all kinds, flooding, and drought. Then look into how this will change in the decades ahead with global warming impacts. Do not rush into buying property to build your village. Make sure you can stay there and grow long term.

Summary Points

- Rural land is the most cost effective approach with the greatest value.
- Rural land is plentiful as most people want to be near the big cities for jobs.

We are what we repeatedly do. Excellence, therefore, is not an act but a habit.

– Aristotle

Village Housing

How to create village housing

The Village startup is recommended at up to ten homes plus a community center. The community center consolidates the initial group. It typically contains two major full bathrooms, laundry room, and a commercial kitchen, along with dining and lounging facilities. It is where the group eats together, particularly dinner. The homes can be smaller because they only need a toilet rather than a full bath, and have a kitchenette rather than a full kitchen. The homes are really detached private spaces for personal activities and sleeping. It can be office space for keyboard warriors and online workers.

This is most efficient if the homes are built around an oval with the community center at one end for easy access. The oval center can be a beautifully landscaped park and dog walk, for example. Individual homes can be as small as 24 x 8' (RV size) up to a more common 32 x 24' two bedroom

house. Unusual houses should be the exception as people can be expected to move on years later. You want the property usable by the village when the current resident leaves.

As the village expands, this pod structure is replicated, perhaps sharing a Community Center in another figure eight configuration. This creates multiple neighborhoods. Additional Community Centers can be smaller. One does need to be large enough to accommodate Village Council Meetings and other full village gatherings.

Start with 5-10 cottages and a community center built around a large oval garden.

With a maximum village size of 200-250 total population, this means you can have four figure eight neighborhoods for a total of 80 homes and four community centers. This all supports an average home of three people or so. This small size limit keeps villages from getting too political. At the least, everyone in the village knows each other well. Many consider the ideal village size to be 50-60 people.

All Village Coops should join the League of New Earth Nations as affiliates, if not full members (Self-Governing Nations). Through New Earth, they can readily trade with other villages all over the world and cross support each other where practical. It is important that each village be financially independent. Then working with others is much easier and minimally political.

Summary Points

- Start with 5-10 cottages and a community center built around a large oval garden.
- Keep the village population small to easily manage. Just create additional villages.

I don’t want to spend my whole life talking about the promised land without ever getting there.

I want to live in it.

- Joyce Meyer

Village Development

What to expect in the long term. Village development timeline.

As villages grow, they go through the three stages of development.

1 **Startup:** Members invest in the village development and establish the community.

2 **Self Sustaining:** The Village net income supports its operating costs.

3 **Financial Interdependence:** The Village generates a financial surplus usable for Member Stipends, Capital Development, new Businesses, and Housing expansion.

1 Startup Stage

Startup is the first two to three years where Members are investing in the development of the village. The adult Members must cover all costs both capital and operations. As previously pointed out, this should run about $500-600 for housing debt per household plus $300-500 per person for community services (food, utilities, etc.). It depends on your budgetary plan.

Capital Costs are those associated with buying the property, building its infrastructure out, and constructing all the housing and buildings, plus any equipment and vehicles needed.

Operational Expenses cover the costs of daily living which typically includes: food, supplies, electronics, transportation, farming supplies, utilities, etc.

Village development is in three stages: 1) Startup Investment 2) Self-sustaining, covering costs, and 3) Financial Independence, building capital

The startup capital also needs to cover the capital requirements of the each income producing business of the village. For rental housing, this means the additional building materials along with the time to put it together. For other businesses, it means the building and equipment needed for the business, and the staff to work it. The foundation business should be started as soon as possible so the village starts earning a surplus to cover expenses quickly.

The non-profit trust at RBEV.org can help you with your initial budgetary planning. There is no cost.

2 Self Sustaining Stage

As the village earns more and more, Member operational expenses can be increasingly reduced. Once operational expenses are readily covered, then reduce the household capital payments assessed, until that reaches zero also. At that point, when the Members need to pay nothing to live in the village, the village itself becomes self sustaining.

A multi-year capital plan is essential to understanding what is possible to do with the earned surplus. Start with an annual operating budget that is given over to the Business Manager(s), the Treasurer and the General Manager to implement. It is reviewed monthly by the village council to be sure they are on track, and updates approved by the Village Council as necessary. It is useful to look out five years to see the impact of various actions on the long term. For example, you can see the impact of building additional buildings sooner on the monthly earnings of the village. You can also see the imp[act of additional businesses you may want to start. It is a useful planning tool you update yearly. It is a starting point for adjusting when big changes happen. It gives a lot of confidence in your plan to all village Members.

> The initial Startup Phase requires investment for land and housing to establish the village.

The annual budget should include anticipated earnings and well as all operational expenses. The loan payments are easily forecasted. As earnings increase, the monthly Member fees can be reduced accordingly. For each yearly planning cycle, decide what to do with the earnings. They can be used for:

- Reducing monthly Member fees (village expenses)
- Reducing monthly Household fees (loan payments)
- Paying Members a cash stipend
- Paying for additional capital for the Village
- Accruing savings for future expansions
- Acquiring companies the village takes over

The annual plan should be lead by the Treasurer as a robust discussion at the Village Council, so that the priorities of all Members may be fully considered. This needs to be a plan the whole village gets behind.

Financial Independence Stage

After a few more years of business development in the Village, it should reach financial independence where it generates much more money that it needs, including development. At this point the excess funds go into a **capital fund** for the Village's use.

This is then used for major new projects such as:

- Starting a new village if needed;
- Starting an additional village business venture;
- Purchasing a business useful to the village;
- Investing in a business at other village;
- Supporting other village startups globally.

Continued business expansion should bring the village to the wealth or capital building phase.

It is also recommended that the Capital Fund be created by a skilled trader to grow it. Investments can be made in equities (stocks, ETFs), currencies (Forex, crypto etc.), Real Estate.

Anyone interested should be able to participate with the trading so they can learn. Day trading and swing trading are two techniques that rely on technical analysis and can produce outstanding returns on capital. Warren Buffet and Kathy Wood offer two different investing approaches that are quite good for the bulk of your fund. These are longer term approaches. Wood looks at company prospects with a five year horizon. Her results are more volitile over ten years. Buffet looks at fundamental value of a business, it's place in the market, and its ability to make money. He does best over ten years with greater consistancy.

Naturally, the results should be reviewed monthly at the Village Council meeting so everyone is aware of what is happening.

Summary Points

- Village development is in three stages: 1) Startup Investment 2) Self-sustaining covering costs, and 3) Financial Independence building capital.
- The initial Startup Phase requires investment for land and housing to establish the village.
- With a good village business, village should be able to pay all bills within a few years.
- Continued business expansion should bring the village to the wealth or capital building phase.

You miss 100% of the shots
you don‟t take.

– Wayne Gretzky

Vehicles & Equipment

Manage village equipment & vehicles collaboratively

Village owned vehicles are the norm. Since most people will not need to work much outside the village, they will need vehicles much less. It is far more cost effective to have a number of vehicles owned by the village and shared. It also reduces the clutter of many vehicles at the village that are just parked. Just schedule them like Zip Cars. The village pays for gas, insurance, and maintenance. Insurance is done on a commercial fleet policy with the vehicle asset trust. We do this. It is surprisingly cheap.

The easiest way to acquire vehicles initially, is for Founding Members who want to do so to offer their cars to the Village. The Village then decides which ones they need and buy them from the owner. If you do not use startup capital for this, or later during development, pay the opwners monthly over a year or two for their car. This car payment could be deducted from the Members monthly operating expense bill initially or put into their Village Trust account later on.

The village, as a community, decides what equipment it needs to buy for its various operations as well. This is incorporated into its annual budget plan. Decide how maintenance will be handled. With enough equipment, and vehicles, a resident repair person may be a good option, if possible. Someone can also be hired to do this for the village. Just plan for it.

Electronics and related services are also provided by the village. Again this is part of the budget plan. Cell phones can be quite cheap on group/family plans.

Have the village pay all bills so members do not need money for daily living.

Similarly tablets and laptops can be provided as needed or desired for recreational personal use.

Computing needed for village business use should also be provided by the village. Of course, all associated services such as WiFi, boosters around the village, etc. are also provided.

Summary Points

- Have the village pay all bills so members do not need money for daily living.
- This includes farm equipment, vehicles and their operation, and electronics such as computing, WiFi, and cell phones

III. Run Your Village

The Red Nation shall rise again and it shall be a blessing for a sick world; a world filled with broken promises, selfishness and separations; a world longing for light again.

- Tȟašúŋke Witkó, Crazy Horse, Oglala Lakota

Village Work

Managing work with village members

As the village grows, the amount of work each person does in support of the village should decrease. Also, people can always be hired to do village or village business work as funds grow. The goal is for people to offer to do work that is fun for them, and make their contribution that way. Over time, free time will grow. Each member should carry an approximately equal workload, as judged by the group. Fairness is critical, of course. No free rides.

If anyone fails repeatedly in their work agreement with the Village Council, they should be banished from the Village swiftly. The village should only carry people (less than full work) with the full agreement of the members, as in the case of someone during sickness or disabled. To do otherwise runs a high risk of alienating all members who quickly determine that commitments are really only guidelines and everyone starts missing their commitments. Be forewarned, this can devolve rapidly – in weeks. It is nearly impossible to reverse.

Similarly, someone who is disruptive to the community should not be tolerated. This is a major behavior issue. This will tear apart a community that is otherwise functioning well. One bad actor undermines the whole structure. They should be put out of the village as quickly as possible, once voted out. It is an extreme response, and so should not be taken lightly. But, realize it can be destructive to the entire village unchecked.

One bad actor can suck the fun out of village life. There are all kinds of bad behaviors from undermining those in responsible positions, to critical talking behind people's backs, to constantly challenging and disagreeing openly with decisions **after** they are made. Nip this in the bud.

> **Especially early on, deal with uncooperative or disruptive members swiftly. They quickly and seriously undermine the village culture.**

The work of the village is according to the Members agreements with the Village Council (each other). This is done by season as workloads vary based on season. It is the output of the work planning session. All the work that will be needed during the upcoming season is listed, people volunteer to take on various tasks, until there is nothing left or no takers. What is untaken must be hired out or not done. If too much work has no takers, and everyone has a full load, the monthly member contribution in the early days needs to be increased. It should be reduced when no longer needed. It is important to get this plan done early so people know what they are committed to do and what is involved.

Summary Points

- The goal is for everyone to do work that is fun for them. Members decide what they will do.
- Members count on each other to fulfill their agreements for work.
- Deal with either uncooperative or disruptive members swiftly. They quickly and seriously undermine the village culture.
- All village work tasks are driven off of a village work plan, collectively created.

A man has two reasons for everything he does: a good one, and the real one.

- J. P. Morgan

Governance

What is the best system for self rule

Village Council

The core operational organization of a Village Coop is the Village Council. It operates like a Board of Directors for Village Operations and for each Village Business. All founding adult members initially form the Village Council. As the village grows, if the meetings get too large and unwieldy, active membership can be restricted. Council Members may be limited in number and elected. However, all Members should be invited to observe in order to maintain transparency and involvement.

A core differentiation in the proposed style of village governance is one based upon "Servant Leadership." In this approach, leaders strive to empower the people they are leading. It is all about responsibility rather than the more conventional authority and power. A leader is not a "Big Boss." They are not the authority. The workers are.

The leaders are merely supervising and coordinating an activity trying to help all the members do the best they can while having fun doing it. This is very different from the typical corporation which is autocratic. Real leaders inspire us. Big bosses tell us. Big difference. Leaders help the work we do be fun, and fit it to our personal needs (at our request).

This is a big difference between Native American Leaders and Western European Managers, often called leaders. Native Leaders always look to the needs of those they are leading. Their best interests are top of mind. What is best for the people? Western European Managers are all about the work and how to get it done most efficiently. People are viewed as production assets, rather than individuals. They even call Personnel "Human Resources" these days to underscore the productive nature of the assets. It's very dehumanizing and demeaning.

The Village Council runs a short meeting weekly to make operational decisions.

The people are the whole point of what you are doing. The Leader is the workers' appointee. People are not a "Human Resource" to be managed as other business assets.

Native tribal chiefs are usually elected by their people. Sometimes they are appointed by the head

Clanswoman. They can be removed if they prove unsatisfactory. The Chief never tells the warriors what to do. He proposed what he thinks they should do. It is then up to each warrior to decide for themselves, or leave the tribe if most agree with the chief, and they cannot go along.

Structure is simple in the initial phases. The Council elects a Chair whose only function is to call and run the meetings. The Council Chair is not a "big boss" but rather just a meeting facilitator. The Village Council Meetings are business meetings.

The Council Meeting approves work plans, budgets, and proposals, reviews progress, approves plan changes, and makes other decisions when needed. It need not be long and wieldy. A good meeting leader will keep discussion tight and on track with the agenda to be sure all the work gets done. Discourage venting and speeches. Agenda topics nearly always arise from a proposal made in advance either written or in a previous meeting, which focuses the discussion on issues needing to be addressed.

A **General Manager** is needed to oversee routine coordination and scheduling of activities, and a **Treasurer** is needed to manage external world finances and purchasing. These positions are elected and chartered by the Village Council for the Village itself.

> **The Village General Manager organizes the tasks to be done running the village.**

If much purchasing is to be done, it is recommended that a Purchasing Manager be designated to assist the Treasurer. This should be someone who is good at finding used (or new) stuff cheap. People who are good at this buy most everything at a price below market. They can turn around and sell it for more. This way the cost to have something is only the cost to use it up, not to acquire it.

For example, if you buy a backhoe or excavator at the right price (early winter), and use it for a year or two, you can then sell if for more in Spring when done with it. It thus costs you nothing to have a backhoe. Most big equipment and tools can be done this way. Do this if you have the capital to tie up.

Village **objectives and budgets** must be defined and approved in advance for each coming year. Once decided, it is up to each manager to implement any way they want, within decided written constraints, to achieve the desired results.

The Treasurer is free to spend each budget line item any way they see fit without further approval except for large capital items. They report monthly to the Village Council and Membership at large on spending vs. plan. There is no second guessing or interference from other Village Members. If Village Members collectively decide a goal is insufficiently defined, they may further define it (usually imposing restrictions on the methods), but never retroactively.

The Village Treasurer manages money and spending with the outside world.

The key is to empower each Member with all they need to accomplish the mission they take on. This allows them to use their creativity and makes the activity fun for them. Members do not perform activities – they accomplish missions (outcomes). Give Members all they need, with reasonable reporting requirements, so they can share with everyone how they are doing.

Policy Governance

The overall governance approach is defined by Policy Governance. This is the overwhelming governance methodology for coops and is well documented. The initial set of Guiding Polices may take some months to develop. It must be sufficiently broad to cover the objective, and allow creativity in solving the issues, yet specific enough to make sure it is going in the direction the Members want.

Remember, once the manager in charge is given the go ahead, they are not messed with. They are free to implement the objective any way they want within the limits of the policies approved. This maximizes empowerment and creativity. Ongoing Guiding Polices tend to get better over time.

The operation of each village business is run by its own General Manager who, like the Village GM, reports to the Village Council. They are independent business entities. The surplus of each business goes into the Village Capital Fund.

Each business General Manager may recruit others to help them with their work. A member so helping gets credit against their village work commitment.

The GM must negotiate this with the Village Council in the general work planning session or propose an amendment to the existing plan. If a new business is proposed during the year, a proposal is needed covering how to fit this with the existing work. There is a whole process covering how to give first choice to existing villagers. Work left undone is then hired out. Villagers always get first dibs on the most fun work.

Here is a sample organization for a Village council:

General Manager: plans and coordinates the work schedule of the Members who are keeping the village running smoothly. This covers food preparation, cooking, meal setup and serving, cleanup and dishes. It also covers routine Community Center cleaning and organizing, show shoveling, landscaping and grounds maintenance, snow plowing, building maintenance, refuse management, village services coordination (like trash pickup), firewood delivery and stacking, and all other tasks associated with running the village. If food growing or animal raising is part of the village food plan, it is included as well. If it is expected to bring in significant revenue, it may be run as a small business, particularly in later years, because the staff needs get substantial. When small, it is gardening or the like, and just another task set.

The Business Manager manages the Village Business for the Village.

Treasurer: Plans and manages the village budget. This includes the overall income and expense for the businesses although the details are managed by those managers. The Treasurer is responsible for having adequate cash on hand to support all planned purchases from outside the village. Asset purchases are done by the Purchasing Manager working under the Treasurer overall. Other members doing routine buying get the funds from the Treasurer (cash or village credit card). Whoever does the transaction provides the receipts to the treasurer for tracking.

Food Manager: If sufficient activity and staff, a separate Food Manager takes care of the planting, growing and harvesting activities, as well as the feeding and raising of the farm animals. There always seems to be a lot to do here so plan carefully. Be careful not to overburden too few Members. They also manage the sales of extra food either to local stores, or through farm stands. They manage on an annual budget which covers all food and material costs as well as income, even if the operation is merely break even. The Food Manager worls under the General Manager for coordination of staff work when food production is relatively small. It can be done either as part of the GM's team or as direct Village Council reporting.

The Farm Manager, when needed, coordinates al the farm related activities.

Rental Manager: Coordinates getting rental customers, administers their stay, and collects payments, whether a few days or many months, sees to their needs, and generally ensures they are well satisfied while there. They provide a point of contact for guests and routinely visit the rental site to check on how things are going. For dominantly monthly rentals that repeat, the work is fairly minimal, but important. Done well, it is the income for the village itself. This can be remarkably profitable. The Rental Manager reports directly to the Village Council.

Other Bus Manager: Other businesses will have a separate business manager with their own budget from the beginning. It may be an online product sales (e.g. book sales, lectures and workshops, online courses, canned preserves, packaged meats, craft products, artistic creations …). They have Members assisting the marketing, social media, product production, packaging, and shipping, and invoicing and collection for the business.

Clearly, Members are the labor pool for each activity area. If there are not Members, then either the activity cannot be done (yet), or outside help must be hired. In the early stages, be careful to not take on too much. The Members must agree with the plan. If the decision is to hire outside people to help, they must be paid, which initially can only come from increased income or the Members raising their monthly costs. This is also a good option for work no one wants to do. For example, the village may hire a janitorial service to clean the Community Center weekly because no one volunteers to do it. It is usuallly assumed that each member is responsible for cleaning their own residence.

Each village business should have its own Business Manager to run the business.

The Village Council is a highly structured operations meeting held weekly. It covers decisions to be made, general work schedule coordination, and a simple financial summary for the week. Since many people like to talk, it is important to be sure everyone is heard on each important decision. Otherwise, issues are not discussed at all. Two members must ratify a proposal for it to be discussed. Members should be encourage to make proposals rather than just "bring up issues." Most all issues should be planned in advance. Avoid supporting people merely making complaints. This also helps keep the meeting short and productive.

To prevent very long meetings with a lot of chit chat, a social hour may be held either before, or preferably after, where people can just talk and express how they feel about various issues and decisions.. It can be challenging to keep the meetings short and interesting. Use handouts for details.

The RBEV.org Village Coop platform has many modules that support this planning and aministrative work. A special version specific to each village is set up on a private server, with training. There is no charge other than cost sharing. This is part of the high tech approach of RBE to bring technology to the work of running a village.

Summary Points

- **The Village Council is a short meeting weekly to make operational decisions.**
- **The Village General Manager organizes the tasks to be done running the village.**
- **The Village Treasurer manages money and spending with the outside world.**
- **The Business Manager manages the Village Business for the Village.**
- **The Farm Manager, when needed, coordinates al the farm related activities.**
- **Each village business should have its own Business Manager to run the business.**
- **Villages use the RBEV.org Village platform application to automate much of the administrative activity.**

Certain things catch your eye, but pursue only those that capture your heart.

- American Indian saying

Village Culture

How to anchor, and preserve your village culture

This book speaks primarily to the initial startup of a village. The rules and principles apply to the Founding Members. All Members are initially involved directly in the running of the village through the Village Council. Each adult Member has one vote, and one equity share, as in any coop.

These Founding Members are the ones who set and anchor the culture and norms of the village. It is important to select them carefully. They set the tone of village living. Villages have gone in many directions. One in Colorado, for example, became an armed militia camp. Another in California became a Christian Community. Your village can go in many directions. Think through what you want. Make sure all your Founding Members are in agreement.

Write out a set of Village Values that are important to you. Agree on what is not important also. For example, how does everyone feel about weapons in the village, open carry? This was a major issue in one village, generating much emotion. Determine what is acceptable as much in advance as you can to prevent problems later. Your initial setup will determine how the village works. It is better to use consensus rather than voting. Voting creates sides that hold positions long after the vote. With consensus, no decision is made until everyone, every single Member, agrees to support the decision, even if they do not favor it. They can live with it.

The Founding Members must carefully set the village culture and values.

The RBEV.org tech platform supports voting on proposals, which is highly encouraged. Someone makes a proposal. Once a second person supports it, everyone's 👍 or 👎 vote gets noted for the discussion at the Village Council meeting. People can also offer comments on other action to take, and concerns to be dealt with in the proposal discussion.

If there are not sufficient interest in the proposal when it arrives at the Council meeting, it may be dropped.

Once established, villages can add members as they desire. It is prudent to bring in new members on a one year probation to be sure they fit within the culture and norms of the village. Also provide a month or two guest rental trial period so people can see if they like living in the village. Do not rush to expand too rapidly. Bring in new people as needed usually for their skills or family closeness.

The maximum size for a village to operate simply is about 200 people including children. As that size is approached, it is time to look to create another village. Consider another village as early as 50-60 Members. During this period, high trust among all members is critical. This is a fragile period of village development. Stability increases with time over the five development years.

Summary Points

- The Founding Members must carefully set the village culture and values.
- Keep the village size under 200 adults so it doesn't get too political.

I salute the light within your eyes
where the whole Universe dwells.

For when you are at that center
within you and I am that place
within me, we shall be one.

- Tȟašúŋke Witkó, Crazy Horse,
Oglala Lakota

Healthcare

How to manage healthcare in a village

Medical care is changing rapidly within the US. People bring whatever coverage they have to the village. Over time, integrative medical care can be provided by members of the village, as well as brought in from outside. Outside medical bills are borne by the Member through whatever medical coverage they have. As of this writing, most everyone can get coverage readily.

The real goal is healthy living, stress free, with healthy food, strong personal practices, and a great village environment. The village can provide most of that. The village is supported by outside medical care both allopathic, natural, and integrative.

Medical needs are trauma, repair, and degenerative disease. The US has outstanding trauma medicine. They are the best in the world for repairing injuries.

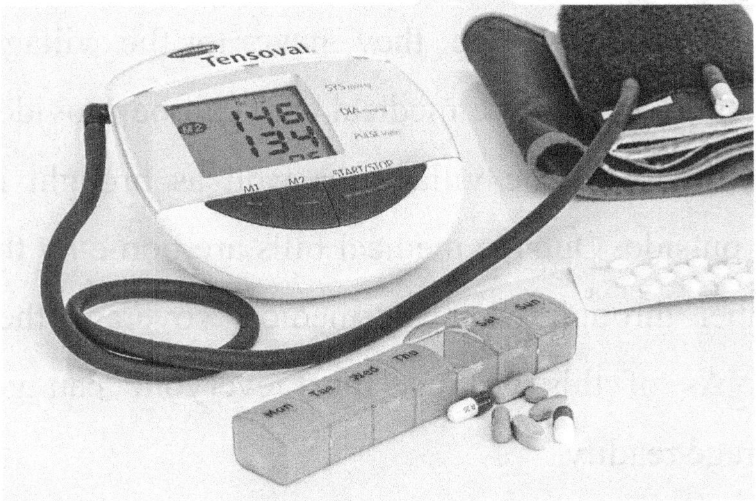

They are also pretty good at repairing defects. This is where external medical coverage is needed. After first aid, it is, and will always likely be, beyond the capability of a village. As a village gets large, a village support plan can be negotiated with external insurance companies limited to what is needed (trauma care).

As people age, disease and degenerative care is the bulk of their medical needs. Sadly, the US lags most of the world in this area. It is dominated by Big Pharma. They see drugs as the solution to all problems.

The village can provide integrative health care and support in addition to members basic healthcare.

US diagnostic testing however is quite strong. Their solutions are what is limited. The approach of allopathic medicine is pretty much "when it breaks, then fix it." Wellness is not the norm. This is why over half of all US MDs are frustrated to the point of quitting. They do not feel they are helping people. They merely relieve symptoms, at best.

A major benefit of a village is the support for a strong healthy lifestyle.

In a village, stress is minimized because people decide on the work they want. They work fairly little, but what they do is fun for them. They actually enjoy it. There are no set hours, just results they know they can get. If the work gets to be too much, others join in to help. They have lots of free time to pursue other interests as well.

Stress is further minimized because there is no money in the village. There is nothing to buy. The Members take care of each other. There is also safety and security in knowing that "The village has got this." Life is easy, fulfilling, and fun. Money is not needed in daily life, just in dealing with the outside world. It is really no more than importing and exporting with other jurisdictions (countries).

By coordinating food and meals, the village can adopt a very healthy sustainable diet. Foods either raised or bought can be organic, free range, and very healthy to eat. Dietary balance can be maintained

Raising much food in the village also contributes to a healthy lifestyle.

with good cooks and planning. Even people who subsist on pizza, burgers and soda will find that slowly over time their bodies will demand better foods. They will find them more and more appetizing. This surprises most people. The cooks need a healthy meal transition plan that the Members agree with. Switching quickly doesn't work. Vegan and meat options are nearly always needed. Again, its up to the villagers to decide together on a plan that accomodates everyone.

With rural living in your own village, exercise and physical activity is relatively easy to maintain. Just walking around the village is exercise in itself. It may not sound like much, but you move around more than in a city home. You tend the crops, feed the animals, let out the goats, etc. There are many physical activities. You will be moving more and being more fit as a result. Everyone has tasks to do that they proposed. No one has a "job."

As you add in Members who are skilled in various healthcare and spiritual practices, you will further enhance the village experience. You can also invite outsiders to visit and share their skills. There are many people who have wellness skills but do not use them full time. In the village they can share them.

Villagers should share their health and wellness skills, and teach their knowledge and skills with others.

Be sure to know what each person can do from Reiki energy work, to therapeutic massage, to guided meditations, to native ceremonies. Do not overlook these activities. They will add considerable depth to your village experience and the wellness of your members.

Also consider sharing your personal knowledge in the form of village talks. Talks are like in-person podcasts. ● They also bring the commuity together. Lifelong learning is a goal for everyone to build their knowledge and skills. This is more than just for home schooling. Adult learning is critical for everyone.

Many healthcare practitioners are also interested in village living, so many, over time, may wish to joinyou. We have been surprised at the number of high level Doctors, Nurses, and Dentists, who are interested in simple village living. Middle age retirement into a village appeals to many of these health care practitioners who can contribute their skills and live much more carefree. They have seen the downside of conventional living. They already get it.

As you build your village, and talk it up, be on the lookout for healthcare workers that can help you and are interested in your village. As you discuss it with those you know, don't be surprised when they express interest.

As they become ready to "retire," commonly by age 50, you can offer them a place in your village. They can start with an office in the village for outsiders (in one of the community centers or build a separate building). Help promote their services locally if they

Many healthcare workers are interested in village living. As the village grows, be on the lookout for them to join you.

need that. Provide administrators who can help them with patients and billing. Alternatively, let them set up their practice outside the village in a nearby location. Have them do some other work in the village, but also service the village itself no charge also in exchange for living in the village. Strike a deal that works for both you and the medical person.

Summary Points

- The village can provide integrative health care and support in addition to members basic healthcare.
- Raising much food in the village also contributes to a healthy lifestyle.
- Villagers should share their health and wellness skills, and teach their knowledge and skills with others.
- Many healthcare workers are interested in village living.As the village grows, be on the lookout for them to join you.

Humankind has not woven the web of life. We are but one thread within it. Whatever we do to the web, we do to ourselves. All things are bound together. All things connect. We are a part of the earth and it is part of us.

- Chief Seattle, Suquamish

Education

How to do education within a village

The global education system is severely behind the times. It was designed for the industrial revolution 150-200 years ago. It has outlived its usefulness. It has become self serving, designed to create more educators and not much else. It has become a world unto itself.

Moreover, with Artificial Intelligence exploding, we can expect the outdated concept of jobs to pretty much vanish by 2030. Anything repetitive will be done by machines. Most people these days are moving into the gig economy anyways. That is what the "Great Retirement" is really all about. The idea of a job is outdated. Who these days, wants to work for a jerk boss, doing boring repetative work, on a fixed schedule, in a fixed location for 40 years! You are just a biological cog in a money making machine.

That said, American public education is particularly weak. Many solutions have been sought with only limited occasional successes. One of the most successful secondary education approaches has been home schooling. There are many support structures all over the country, and online, to assist families in doing this. Home schooled children tend to do better in life than the public schooled.

Thus, village education can be best accomplished through home schooling in conjunction with local school systems in nearby communities. The exact way a village structures this depends on the number and ages of the children, and the proximity of appropriate public schooling.

In the beginning, if there are not enough adults to accomplish home schooling, using a nearby public school may be the only choice. It can, of course, be supplemented with some home schooling and online learning.

Home schooling is a great alternative to public schooling. It works well.

This is particularly valuable if the other Members in the village participate in areas they are passionate about. Members are encouraged to do talks and share wisdom with other members in areas of their expert knowledge. Promote learning. Make it fun.

The RBEV.org admin platform has a home schooling module that is quite strong, and can support your efforts.

This can cover primary and secondary education up through high school. Beyond that, each child should have some college or apprentice experience leading to a profession or skill set that they are drawn to.

The Croatan Oyate tribe has a college and graduate school relationship with Sias International University in China, so members can go to college at very low cost (~$4,000 tuition, village paid) and study abroad. Room and Board are cheaper than living in the US by far ($2-2,500/year). At Sias, a large university in Zhengzhou, they will rub shoulders with the future leaders of the Eastern World, learn dominantly in English, and naturally learn Chinese (Mandarin). They will also learn much more than the limited perspective of American schools. They will get a truly global perspective.

> **For advanced education look to Asian and other Universities for cost effective training along side future world leaders.**

There are other international universities around the world that are similarly more cost effective than American Universities. They provide cultural, language, and social education as well as formal studies. Asian Universities are growing particularly fast with international students, as the US drops off. Just don't forget the backgrounds and experience of your village members. They can do talks on what they know. They can share their wisdom. They can teach skills and languages.

Encourage hands on learning and apprentice style programs for younger people, or anyone wanting to learn something new. Learn under a master. Eventually open your programs to people from other villages. When villages collaborate together, they can share members who want to earn new skills and knowledge. It can be an amazingly enriching environment.

Summary Points

- Home schooling is a great alternative to public schooling. It works well.
- For advanced education look to Asian and other Universities for cost effective training along side future world leaders.

Those who cannot change their minds,
cannot change anything.

- George Bernard Shaw

Village Security

How to maintain security within a village

Your village may get large enough so that it starts to need its own security, particularly for dealing with the public. Think of your village coop as at least its own town. You can also share security with other villages.

RBEV.org is prepared to help you set up your own formal police force if you desire, and help you connect it to the surrounding police forces for backup and support. You may only need one or two officers most of the time. It is best to start with a villager with law enforcement or sometimes if appropriate military training. But backup from local county and nearby municipal police is good for big events. Perhaps your village puts on a large concert or similar big public function.

Nearby police groups like to do this in the US. Since you will likely be more remote, perhaps up in the mountains, you can be on scene there faster than the locals who come from the towns. It's an easily made backup agreement. In addition, it is supported by the state Attorneys Generals because they get additional federal funding if they support an additional police force, even if it is outside their jurisdiction (e.g. Canadian police on the US-Canada border or Native American tribal police).

When you develop a police force, you will also need a court system for at least simple offenses, particularly those that the local jurisdiction will not adjudicate. For example, you may have stronger environmental offenses that a rural county.

A common way to create a judiciary is to create an Elder Council of elected wise seniors in the Village who are not already Village Council Members or want something different. The Village Council is basically the Executive Branch. The Elder council is the Judicial Branch.

You can setup your own police force when you get larger. Connect with local police departments for support.

Early on, if you wish to initiate this, the work can be done by the Village Council in special Judiciary Sessions.

To add formality and seriousness to your proceedings, it is advisable to borrow a nearby county's Council Chambers when not in use. Most are amenable to this practice. Also buy judicial robes for the Elders so they look the part, particularly for visitors to the village.

One common way to bring charges is to have this done by the Village Police Chief who brings the charges before the Elder Council as the prosecutor. The Village General Manager or other senior Member, then takes the side of the defendant in the action before the Elders. His job is to be sure the charges are kept to real violations of the village principles and are not tainted by the personality of the defendant,

especially if the defendant has been annoying or disruptive.

The role of the Elder Council is to hear the evidence and determine if the spirit of one or more core village values have been violated. If that is the case, they then also decide what the repurcussions should be.

When the need arises, create a judicial group to try offenses, particularly with visitors and guests.

It may be a fine, banishment, community service, or any other sentence that they think will help the defendant to take the values seriously and not further repeat violations. They may also turn the defendant over to the local jurisdiction for further prosecution by them when the offense is particularly grievous. As you can imagine, this can easily get out of hand.

Village Court is useful for dealing with Member violations that are repeated or severe where banishment from the village is a likely option. Early on, special community service may be a good option. Another category of offense are visitors who disregard the values of the village in a serious way. Of course, a warning should first be given to ensure the visitor is aware that their behavior is offensive to the villagers. It is all a function of what is important to the village.

It is important to not fall into the western trap of "rule of law." Instead, use the wisdom of the village Elders to examine behavior and determine if someone willfully violated the principles of the village. Replace convoluted rules and ordinances with sound judgement. Remember, the goal is to prevent future bad behavior rather than punish bad past behavior. As you can see, it is truly possible to live in "your own country."

Use a restorative justice approach to handling offenses.

You can have it your way!

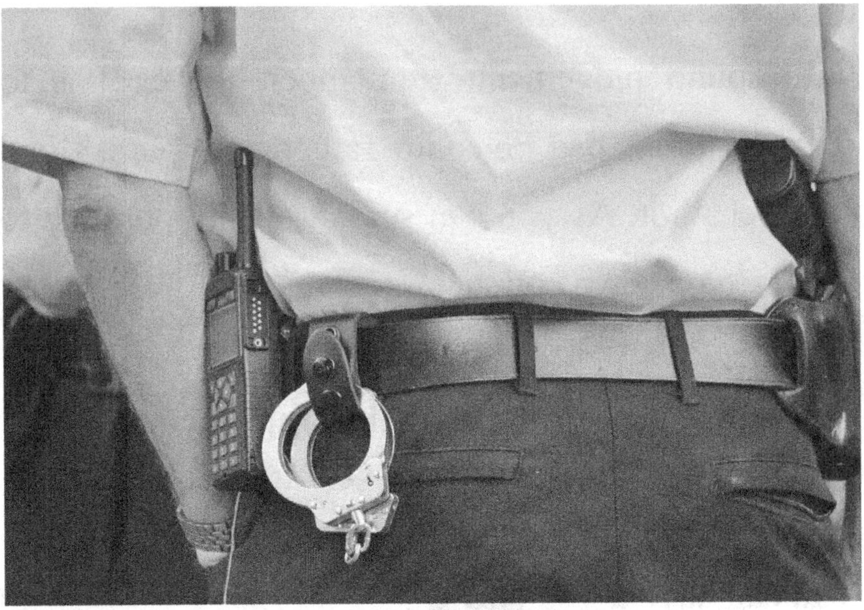

Summary Points

- You can setup your own police force when you get large enough. Connect with local police departments for support.
- When the need arises, create a judicial group to try offenses, particularly with visitors and guests.
- Use a restorative justice approach to handling offenses.

Twenty years from now you will be more disappointed by the things you didn't do than by the ones you did.

– Mark Twain

Long Term Planning

How to routinely plan for future decades

It takes many people to make a village. Be open to all who can contribute. It is just a question of striking a balance between what you want and what you can "afford." We cannot do everything all at once. We recommend you keep several lists of Opportunities.

1. **Village Desires:** what you want to add into the village. Determine the conditions that are needed to include it into the plan. Determine the resources that will be required. Prioritize on this list. This can be things you acquire, activities you do, and skills/people you seek. If something is important,

never say "No." Say "Not Now." Then decide where it fits on your list, its priority.

2. **Business Opportunities:** You will likely have far more business ideas for ways the village can make money than you have people or capital to do them. As AI develops, work will be more and more creative and inter-personal (coaching). Creative can be making things, creating experiences, and artistic expression in its many forms. Empathy will become highly valued as people do not like to interface directly with machines. Other people will be the main interface to people seeking services. These will all be increasingly valuable. The machines will take over the drudgery and repetitive work for us. We get to do the fun stuff relating and helping people and creating new things with minimal effort.

In a coop village, you not only get to do work you love, but you get the benefits as the owner of all the profits generated. This is in sharp contrast to conventional business where the workers continue to get the minimul possible to pay, while the corporation gets the profits.

Keep a prioritized list of potential future business opportunities and leaders.

First, for each idea, require a written proposal that everyone can review. This will show how much capital will be needed over time. It will also show how many people/skills are needed and how much of their labor. With this it should show the estimated surplus from business operations over time returned to the village. Have village members who can help others develop their proposals. A critical element is, of course, a Member with the skills and passion to really drive the development of the proposed business. Don't invest in concepts. Know-how is valuable. Have a strong plan and a passionate leader.

Review each of these lists periodically and keep them fresh, reflecting the desires of the Members. Never discard an idea or proposal. Put it on the list in priority order. If deficient, identify what is needed to be viable – key leader, key skills, etc. Have the proposal list available to the Members, preferably online, with someone in charge of keeping it updated.

Be sure to provide resources to Members to help them flesh out their concepts into business proposals. Rbev.org has templates for business planning that can assist in doing this work. Few people are actually good at assessing business opportunities. You should have at least one in your village from the start. You can set up a portfolio review team if you have several. The idea is to get the best ideas with the best plans. This way you avoid costly mistakes investing in a business, with capital, labor, and time only to find it doesn't work well. A little planning can go a long way here.

If you keep the processes in developing the village open to all, you will bring others along as you grow. They will develop the skills and experience to do it themselves. Apprentice those with strong interest, with others with strong skills, so they can learn. This is where future village leaders come from.

Summary Points

- Keep a prioritized list of potential future business opportunities and leaders.

The Red Nation shall rise again and it shall be a blessing for a sick world; a world filled with broken promises, selfishness and separations; a world longing for light again.

- Crazy Horse, Oglala Lakota Sioux

New Earth Nations

A network for collaborating with other village communities

A village may rise to the level of a small nation or micro-nation wherein it may join The League of New Earth Nations as a Member nation. New Earth Nations is a United Nations like organization where small micro-nations may consolidate their combined economic power, and trade resources among themselves. Actually it is patterned after the League of Nations (simpler).

New Earth Nations is a member of the Well-being Economic Alliance of countries and cities. Unlike the United Nations which is based on military security, New Earth Nations is based on Economics, Trade, and Commerce.

New Earth Nations is currently formally based in Montreal but operates worldwide. Any self-governing village may apply to join, and few are rejected. The only hard requirement is to sign the New Earth Nations Covenant.

Summary Points

- New Earth Nations is a way for Villages to coordinate and collaborate worldwide.

About The Author

Wašaka is Chief (Itančan) of the Croatan Oyate, a tribal nation, and chairs the Tribal Council. He is an experienced business leader and CFO, Speaker, Writer, and a consultant on Board Governance and Sovereign Common Law Trusts. Wašaka only has that one name but legally uses Itančan (Chief) as his "first" name for simplicity with form filling.

He is also a Trustee of RBE Villages, a nonprofit that helps startup rural villages with best practices, strategy and capital planning support, on-site construction assistance, and guidance to achieve financial independence, and sovereignty where desired. Trustees are from Business, the Small Business Administration, Ubuntu USA, plus Mashantucket Pequot and Croatan Oyate Tribal Nations.

Wašaka has provided business consulting services through 1st Venture Partners, a Tribal Trust, since 1994. His focus is on entrepreneurial development, environmental construction, renewable energy, and community organizations.

Wašaka has a strong entrepreneurial and corporate business background. He worked for nearly three decades at a computer company running several divisions with annual revenues over $7 billion. He has also been CEO of a Renewable Energy Company, a Franchising Consultant, a Franchise Development Director, CFO for a Restaurant Group, and CEO of a Tour Company.

Prior to a career in business, he worked as a Theoretical Physicist in Albuquerque NM, contributing optics equations work on the Lunar Excursion Module, and equation analysis of Nuclear Blast EMPs.

He serves on many Boards and has for decades. As an expert in Board Governance, he usually contributes on Organizational Strategy, Financial Strategy, Governance, and Director Training. He is also a member of the CFO Network.

International Speaking Engagements

- May 2018: Keynote Speaker at 1st Inaugural International Education Summit in Zhengzhou China. Spoke on job creation and an educational approach to engage young people today.
- Oct 2017: Spoke at United Nations World Energy Forum as Indigenous Head of State, on Renewable Energy as Chief of native tribe, Croatan Oyate Tribal Nation.

Married to Leslie Mountain Flower Hammond (Taos Pueblo tribe), CEO of Global Wisdom. They live in New London CT and Taos Pueblo NM.

Author: Build Your Village; Sovereign Trusts: A Handbook For Tribes; Power Business Plans; Jump Start Your Business: An Analytic Approach To Business Modeling; Get More Clients; and Lathrop State Park Treasures. Books in development: Croatan Nation History; Thrive & Flourish: Why Create Your Own Community.

Personal Interests:

- Boater and sailor
- Day & Swing Trader: Equities
- Master SCUBA Diver (PADI certified)
- Kayaking expedition leader
- Licensed SCCA Road Racing driver - retired
- Hang glider pilot - retired

Itančan Wašaka (Chief Strong)
ItancanWasaka@gmail.com
iPhone: 860-389-1890
New London, CT and Taos Pueblo, NM

When all the trees have been cut
down, when all the animals have been
hunted, when all the waters are
polluted, when all the air is unsafe to
breathe, only then will you discover
you cannot eat money.

- Cree Prophecy

DREAM BIG
&
MAKE IT HAPPEN

Books From Pueblo Press

Conversational Intelligence

by Leslie Karen Hammond

A practical guide to understanding the dynamics of effective communication.

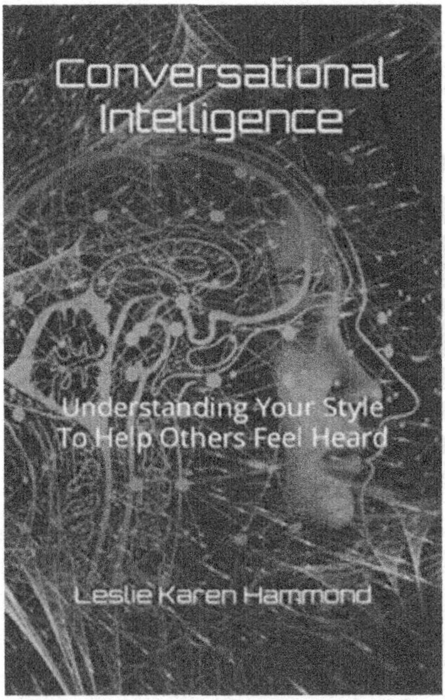

How different would your life be if people understood you and you were clear about what you heard? Misunderstandings provide extraordinary teaching moments.

This book offers tools to discover what's behind the way you communicate to understand better why everyone else shows up in the world the way they do. Once you see how your stories shape you, everyone else will begin to make more sense.

Holding Space

by Leslie Karen Hammond

Leslie's fourth book - Holding Space refers to the

creation of an energetic environment of possibility. It's an intention always set for the highest good of all involved regardless of opinion, experience, or dogma. When you hold space without getting attached emotionally to any particular outcome, the most surprising things happen.

Holding Space

by Leslie Karen Hammond

Leslie's third book - Keep It Real is an invitation to understand what keeps people silent. Readers are guaranteed to gain a profound sense of self in addition to developing compassion for those who remain silent.

Through Leslie's journey of finding, losing, and regaining her voice, she's developed a unique perspective on worthiness.

Women Rising

by Leslie Karen Hammond

Leslie's second book – Women Rising is an invitation to see your journey, up until this point, in a new light. Women are capable of embracing their past and appreciating it as the foundation of who they are today.

Every story has the ability to empower or deflate the spirit. When life events are transformed from pain into teaching moments it's easier to let go of the past and forge ahead.

Leslie's first book – Tap Your Source is a guide to manage your way through the major transitions life throws at you from job changes to the loss of a loved one. The exercises within help you get to the source of where your true self dwells.

Holding Space

by Leslie Karen Hammond

Leslie's first book – Tap Your Source is a guide to manage your way through the major transitions life throws at you from job changes to the loss of a loved one. The exercises within help you get to the source of where your true self dwells.

Lathrop Treasures

by **Itančan Wašaka**

A photo documentary of the natural beauty found at Lathrop State Park near Walsenburg Colorado. The photos were taken by Kimimela Wachichi. TheAmerican Indian quotes are provided by Wašaka.

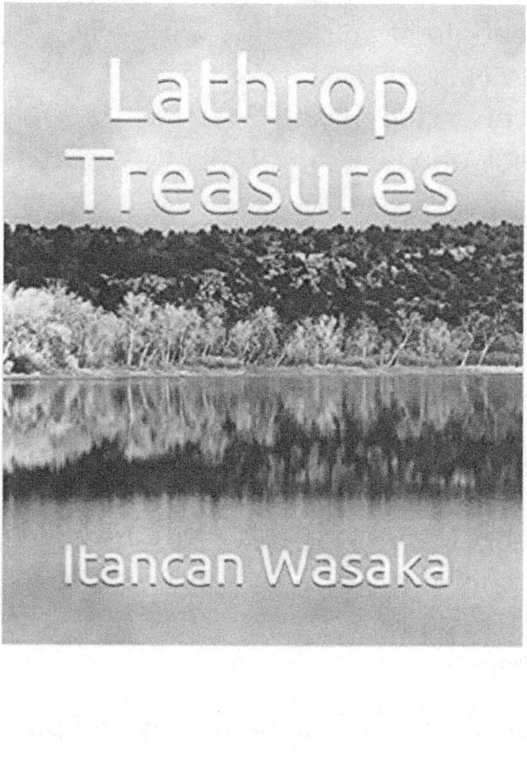

Sovereign Trusts: Handbook For Native Tribes

by Itančan **Wašaka**

This handbook is for tribes that have established themselves, and their tribal trust, using the United Nations Declaration of the Rights of Indigenous People. It helps understand how to maintain tribal jurisdiction when all US the various jurisdictions work to acquire jurisdiction over the tribe. This is an advanced book and requires a familiarity with Sovereign Trust law and US Jurisdictions.

Sovereign Trusts is available in hard copy and paperback.

Notes

Made in the USA
Monee, IL
04 November 2026

67384744R00157